ALBRECHT DÜRER
DIARY OF HIS JOURNEY
TO THE NETHERLANDS 1520 1521

ACCOMPANIED BY THE SILVERPOINT SKETCHBOOK
AND PAINTINGS AND DRAWINGS MADE
DURING HIS JOURNEY

WITH AN INTRODUCTION BY J.-A. GORIS AND G. MARLIER

LUND HUMPHRIES LONDON

First English language edition 1971
Published by
Lund Humphries Publishers Limited
12 Bedford Square London WC1

SBN 85331 283 4

Publishers' note :

The Diary itself is reproduced from Lord Conway : *The Literary Remains of Albrecht
Dürer*, Cambridge University Press 1889, by kind permission of the publishers.
The introduction, notes to the Diary, and list of illustrations, edited by Dieter
Kuhrmann, have been translated from the French by Philip Troutman, Curator,
Courtauld Institute Galleries, London, and Suzanne Alexander.

Made and printed in Belgium

CONTENTS

INTRODUCTION

ON THE 12TH JULY 1520 ALBRECHT DÜRER, AC-
companied by his wife Agnes Frey and maid-servant Susanna, left
Nuremberg for the Netherlands, where he was to spend just under
one year.   A number of things appear to have motivated this ambitious
journey.   In particular, Dürer wished to meet the young Emperor
Charles, from whom he hoped to have confirmed the annual pension
granted him by the late Emperor Maximilian.   However, the artist
would not have stayed so long in the Netherlands had it not been
that the journey was primarily conceived as a business trip.   In
fact, during his stay in Antwerp, Dürer was mainly concerned in
securing the sale of his "books" of wood-cuts and his individual
engravings.   Also, in the summer of the year 1520, the plague had
come to Nuremberg, and it was possibly for this reason that the
painter took with him his wife and maid-servant.

The Diary which Dürer compiled during the twelve months of his
absence from Nuremberg is neither a simple narrative of his impres-
sions on the journey nor a detailed description of the sights he
witnessed.   It is, in effect, a very precise ledger in which the artist
noted his expenses down to the last farthing: his travelling expenses,
the cost of board and lodging, the various purchases he made, the
money he lost at gambling or spent at the cabarets and spas.   And
with the same care he recorded everything that could properly be
considered as gains, that is to say the sums derived from the sale of
his own paintings, drawings and engravings, in that order of importance as far as his receipts are concerned. Sometimes the artist would
barter his works, exchanging a set of his engravings for some *objet
d'art* or other object.   Dürer also kept a detailed account of the
various gifts he made or received.   Briefly, the Diary appears to be
essentially a ledger setting out receipts and expenses, and keeping
the painter informed of the financial state of his venture during his
stay in the Netherlands.

Besides the purely financial data, Dürer could not avoid making a
number of observations on what he had seen in the Netherlands.
Thus, he describes at some length the great procession he witnessed
in Antwerp; or again, the treasures brought from Mexico that he
saw exhibited at the Palace in Brussels.   Further on, he relates in
somewhat pompous fashion the serious risks he took in Zeeland ;
and shortly before his return he suddenly interrupts his book-keeping
to improvise a pathetic lament on the tragedy of Luther and
Christianity.

The Diary of his journey also tells us in a very direct way much
about Dürer's character.   It tells us what were the painter's reactions

towards the men, artists, places, monuments and works of art he encountered in the Netherlands. It provides us, too, with invaluable information on the German master's method of working and on the way in which he organised the sale of his works. The Diary shows us Dürer intimately, stripped of artificiality and pretence. We find him sensitive to the flattering welcome of his Netherlandish colleagues; thus, he records with appealing naïvity the many marks of appreciation and admiration showered upon him in the various towns of the Low Countries. In the light of the Diary, Dürer's character appears to have been full of contrasts. On the one hand, we see a pious, extremely thrifty man who records his every expense to the last farthing, and on the other hand, a man indulging in lavish spending on all manner of useless if intriguing objects. As a passionate collector he bought the oddest of things, apparently intended to enrich his cabinet of curiosities. The list of these purchases evokes the strangest collection of bric-a-brac imaginable: there are buffalo horns, eland's hooves, tortoises, parrots, little dried fishes, bamboo canes, sea-shells, gems, etc... Anything exotic made a special appeal: the treasures brought back by the Spanish adventurers from Mexico and exhibited at the Palace in Brussels plunged him into such ecstasy that he could not find words to express his admiration. This last fact is significant: it tells us how Dürer's spirit was moved when faced with the unknown, whether it was something from some distant land or from some past time. In Antwerp, what he admired above all, apart from the Church of Notre-Dame and the Abbey of Saint Michael, were the bones of the legendary giant. Finally, as soon as he learns that a whale has been washed up on the shore in Zeeland, he can hardly contain himself and sets out from Antwerp for Ziericksee, in the middle of the winter, travelling on horseback to Bergen-op-Zoom and thence by boat to Goes, Veere and Arnemuide.

In addition to what the Diary tells us about Dürer, it is also a document of immense value for an understanding of the customs, ideas and artistic life in the Netherlands during the time of the Reformation. Historians of Netherlandish art have found it, indeed, a source of greater importance than the richest of archives. The original manuscript of the Diary of the journey to the Netherlands is lost, but its text has been handed down in two copies whose authenticity is hardly to be questioned. One of the copies, known as "Manuscript A", is preserved in the Bamberg Library; the other, and older copy, "Manuscript B", is in the Nuremberg State Archives.

CHAPTER I   9

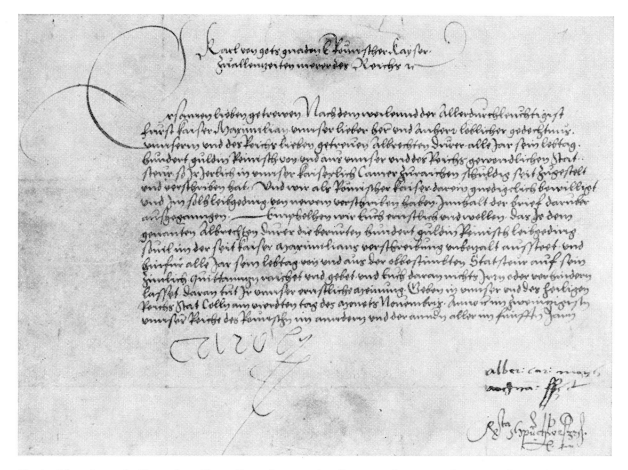

Charles V's order to the Nuremberg Town Council concerning the grant of an Imperial pension of 100 Rhenish florins to Albrecht Dürer.   Town Archives, Nuremberg.

CHAPTER I

ON THE 20TH JUNE 1520, POPE LEO X ISSUED against Dürer the Bull of Excommunication, the *Exsurge Domine*, which ends the first phase of the reformer's rebellion against the authority of Rome. A month later, Albrecht Dürer was on his way to the Netherlands. He was leaving a Germany deeply disturbed by theological disputes. Clear-sighted minds already had premonitions of the deep social and political tumult that was to be provoked by the religious conflicts.

At this time the Lutheran reform had not strictly speaking begun: it was more a question of a "movement" in which a general sense of protestation was of more importance than dogmatic formulae which would allow a new Church to be formed. But this movement seemed to gather together a considerable number of leading thinkers, scholars, philosophers and artists. Dürer was among the sympathisers. As early as 1518 he had given Luther a token selection of his engravings. The latter thanked him, and in his letter appears to refer to the famous engraving "The Knight, Death and the Devil". In 1519, Jan van Scorel confirms that Dürer is a Lutheran [1]. During his stay in the Low Countries the painter does not hide his admiration for Luther, and expresses in pathetic terms his grief and fears when Luther is arrested and taken under escort to the Wartburg. In the Netherlands, and more particularly in Antwerp, Dürer was to find an atmosphere strongly resembling that which reigned in central Germany, especially at Ulm, Nuremberg and other towns won over to the Reformation. He was to find consciences rudely shaken by the great wave of revolt and forebodings, and ecclesiastical institutions heavily compromised by abuses and by the collusion of the temporal and spiritual, manifestly illustrated by the traffic in indulgences. He was to come into contact with a circle of philosophers who, under the influence of Erasmus, had broken with scholastic thought and all other forms of medieval thinking. In Antwerp he was to witness the spiritual and material unrest which was a prelude to the great revolutionary ideas which marked the modern capitalist era.

Antwerp was entering a decisive phase of its history. She had amply benefited from the economic decadence of Bruges, and through the sovereigns' protection had increased the lead she had gained in 1488 over all other towns of the Low Countries. She had received within her walls the colonies of foreign merchants who controlled international commerce and who for nearly a century previously had been established in Bruges. The Portuguese colony was particularly important at the time of the discovery of America and had set the example of

[1] W. WAETZOLDT. - *Dürer und seine Zeit*, Vienna, 1935.

CHAPTER II   11

settling in Antwerp as early as 1510. The Italians, Spaniards, English and Germans followed. This foreign population, rich, active and productive, was perhaps not so important numerically in a town of 100,000 inhabitants, but the few hundred international merchants and financiers were quite sufficient to give the city a cosmopolitan atmosphere and introduce a new spirit into the town at the close of the Middle Ages.

As opposed to Bruges and other Netherlandish towns, the presence in Antwerp of an economic and religious liberalism was soon to give the town its greatness and display its weaknesses, the effect of which was to continue far into the sixteenth century. An agreement was made between the Bishop of Cambrai and the Magistrate of Antwerp to protect the city from a too severe application of the enactments of the Inquisition and the Emperor. Her policies consisted of separating the temporal from the spiritual and she firmly rejected interference in her affairs from the central authority. She knew how to take radical measures whenever her commercial interests were threatened: thus, to avoid conflict, divine worship was to be suspended during the fortnight of the town's fair. Wherever governmental policy threatened the town's material interests, she was to bring to bear her cosmopolitan spirit which could neither understand nor tolerate any rigid application of the law (¹).

The "anticlerical" feeling, which throughout the sixteenth century inspired the town's approach to its commercial administration, was also excellent ground for the propagation of Lutheran ideas. The most famous adherent of the Reformation movement was Cornelis Grapheus, Communal Secretary and a prolific writer, as well as historian, poet and orator. His highly important administrative functions afforded him considerable authority and influence, and his writings added to his prestige. Dürer was to be on friendly terms with him. When the painter came to make his farewells, Grapheus presented him with a copy of one of Luther's short treatises, "*Von der Babylonischen Gefengknuss der Kirchen*" (Babylonian Captivity), as his parting gift. Some months later, Cornelis Grapheus attended the burning of Luther's books in the Grande Place. On the 6th May 1521 he had solemnly to renounce at the altar of the Church of Notre-Dame the Lutheran heresies which in his capacity of poet and historian he had propagated (²).

Dürer also met Peter Gillis (³), Clerk of the Court of the town, who had been one of Erasmus' friends and whom the philosopher mentions in his "Adages" as having been his host. There is nothing to prove that Gillis was a Lutheran, but he certainly belonged to

(¹) J.-A. Goris. - *Etude sur les colonies marchandes méridionales (Portugais, Espagnols, Italiens) à Anvers de 1488 à 1567*, Louvain, 1925.

(²) Mertens and Torfs. - *Geschiedenis van Antwerpen*, vol. IV passim.

(³) *Ibidem*.

CHAPTER II

the circle of Grapheus and Proesten, the Prior of the Augustines, to be mentioned later, both ardent adherents of the Reformation.

But the painter's constant companions and everyday friends were the members of the Portuguese colony, the commercial representatives of the King of Portugal, who were known as "factors" and were among the most important members of the foreign community and commercial world of Antwerp. The Portuguese "factor" also received from his master specific authority to spend any moneys or to purchase any quantities of goods on behalf of the Crown of Portugal ([1]).

([1]) GUICCIARDINI. – *Description de tous les Pays-Bas, passim.*

At the time of Dürer's arrival in Antwerp, the agency was in the hands of Francisco Pesão, assisted by Rodrigo Fernandez. Dürer knew these two men and mentions them in his Diary, confusing their titles. However, his best friend was their successor, João Brandão, who held the post of factor on a number of occasions and became factor for the second time in October 1520. Brandão was one of the most able agents in the Portuguese service. Dürer made his portrait and also those of his secretary and his Moorish servant.

Paul Kalkoff tried to establish that these Portuguese agents were Maronites, or *Marronos*. This appellation applied to the Portuguese Jews who were converted to Christianity by force at the end of the fifteenth century and who, whilst showing all outward signs of being Catholics, remained faithful to their original convictions. They were suspected of being in favour of the Reformation, whose apparent tolerance was in any event welcome to them. In Germany their true religious feelings were known : in 1519, a Lutheran treatise, printed in Wittenberg, symbolised their equivocal attitude in the person of the *Moranus exul* who followed Charles V's entry into Antwerp ([2]). Aleander, the delegate of the Pope responsible for applying the bull *Exsurge Domine*, accused them openly of fermenting religious disturbance in Antwerp. After Dürer's departure, Aleander's opinion was that the attitude of the foreign merchants was impeccable, but he makes exception in the case of the German merchants and a few Maronites.

([2]) P. KALKOFF. – *Die Anfänge der Gegenreformation in den Niederlanden*, Halle, 1903-1904.

In July 1521, their community bore the cost of publishing Luther's works in Spanish, which entered into Spain through devious channels. Aleander suggested that "half-a-dozen Lutherans should be burnt alive and have their property confiscated". It is not known however whether or not the leading Portuguese merchants, whose company Dürer sought and with whom he was in regular contact, were Maronites. It is possible but perhaps unlikely. In any event, there is no evidence either way and certain details tend to reject the possibility: thus Brandão had been one of the local officers responsible for the collection of the taxes imposed on the Maronites at Oporto.

It is nevertheless unlikely that Dürer, who was a fervent admirer of Luther and in close contact with the adherents of the Reformation in Antwerp, would have sought the close friendship of and intercourse with people whose responsibilities and social position made them honour bound to respect Imperial policies. No doubt the Portuguese agents, knowing the Maronites whom the Portuguese community wanted to absorb at any price, felt neither distrust nor hostility towards them. There is, however, no trace of any dealings on the part of Dürer with the Portuguese Jews, whose descendants and successors were to be the object of spectacular religious proceedings in Antwerp during the first half of the sixteenth century.

Dürer was also in contact with the Augustine Prior, Jacob Proesten, a student and ardent disciple of Luther and one of the most vigorous defenders of Lutheranism in Antwerp. His monastery preached against indulgences; and attendance at the church was so great that special stands had to be erected. Proesten left Antwerp at the time Dürer was staying there and went to Wittenberg, where he was made Bachelor in Theology, on the 13th May 1521, and Licentiate, on the 12th July. Luther had a great liking for him and called him "the fat little Fleming" ("*der fette kleine Flaming*"). In 1522, he was convicted of heresy and had to forswear before Cardinal Aleander. He returned to his heretical beliefs and finally escaped to Germany where he died. It is beyond doubt that the whole Augustine order had embraced Lutheranism. After Proesten's departure, Dürer was to continue his visits to the monastery. It goes without saying that Dürer would have sought the company of his compatriots living in Antwerp. Aleander regarded all the German merchants as heretics.

It is, then, established that everyone, with the exception of the artists whose company Dürer sought, were ardent supporters of the Reformation. Accordingly it is not surprising that some writers have tried to establish a connection between Dürer's departure from Antwerp and the arrival in the town of Cardinal Aleander, whose activities led to the arrest of some of the most eminent of the artist's friends. It may be tempting to believe this was the case but there is no real evidence to support the supposition.

There remains for us to discuss the relationship of the painter with the most famous of all the humanists, Erasmus, to whom Dürer addressed the exhortation in his Diary. Dürer tells us, without further comment, that he had dined with Erasmus and had drawn

CHAPTER II

his portrait; but when news of Luther's arrest at the Diet of Worms reached Antwerp, the Diary, remarkable otherwise for its laconic and prosaic factual record, becomes extraordinarily eloquent. It contains a particularly curious passage which throws a very special light on the painter's psychological state and on Erasmus' character. Dürer exhorts the great man to take up his pen and continue without delay the work begun by Luther, whom he believes to have been assassinated by the enemies of the Reformation. He offers Erasmus the palm of martyrdom, and seeks to convince him with a remarkably peremptory argument, but one that was nevertheless pointed, in view of the person to whom it was directed: "...thou givest thyself but two more years", he tells Erasmus, "lay out the same for the good of the Gospel and of the true Christian faith... and if thou sufferedst infamy and didst die a little sooner then wouldst thou be glorified in Christ".

It is not known if Erasmus read this apocalyptical text. Did it remain simply a confidence written to relieve an anguished soul? One knows Erasmus' reactions to exhortations, made from all quarters, that he take up a stand in the Lutheran affair. He was at the time in Anderlecht, whence he addressed some twenty letters which are still preserved and which witness the troubles and difficulties which harassed him ([1]). The Catholics incited him to enter the lists against Luther, although he had not even had time to read the prolific writings of the Reformer, absorbed as he was in the preparation of his own edition of the New Testament and other philological works. His enemies in the Catholic camp "bellowed" at him and denounced him to the Princes. He even believed himself to be threatened by the sword or poison. "It is clear to everyone", he writes, "that these people will dare anything." The Lutherans reproached him, as did Dürer, with betraying the good cause and with destroying through his waverings and lack of frankness the work of reform which he himself had so courageously undertaken.

In a letter to Daniel Tayspil of Neuve-Eglise, Erasmus reports the disappearance of Luther as a news item, of importance no doubt but one which did not move him in any way. He relates the fact without comment. This indifference is in startling contrast to the vehement indignation and despairing laments that Dürer confides to us in his Diary.

Had Erasmus known this passage, he would have replied with a categorical "*non-possumus*" to Dürer's admonitory waving of the palm of martyrdom before him. This humanist scholar aspired to no such honour : "I should choose to be Christ's martyr if Christ

([1]) M. C. SOBRY. - *Les vingt-deux lettres d'Erasme écrites à Anderlecht en 1521. (Bulletin du Service de Recherches historiques et folkloriques du Brabant.)*, Brussels, June 1936.

himself gave me the strength to be one", he writes later to Ulrich von Hutten, "but I should not want to be Luther's martyr." Erasmus imagined the Germans wanted him to be implicated by fair means or foul in the "Lutheran affair". The result, he explained, would have been that : "Instead of a single victim there would have been two". He definitely did not feel that he had : "the qualities needed to go so far as to risk one's life fighting for the truth. Not all of us have sufficient strength to bear martyrdom." He disapproves of Luther and emphatically denies authorship of the anti-Catholic tracts which were attributed to him by Aleander. He did not want to be involved in quarrels at any price. Both Luther's enemies and followers tried to draw him to their side, but : "None of that was to shake me or make me relinquish my intentions". With considerable foresight he predicts the consequences of the "Lutheran tragedy", which were to destroy the peace of nations, especially that of the Netherlands.

CHAPTER II

DÜRER'S RELATIONSHIP WITH THE ARTISTS OF THE Low Countries is of paramount importance in the study of Netherlandish painting of the first decades of the sixteenth century. For a long time this factor was effectively ignored, attention being directed more exclusively to his connection with Italian art, the importance of which was perhaps over-emphasised. In any event, many other questions, no less decisive, were overlooked. For some time there has been a truer conception of Dürer's influence. Many writers came to appreciate the contribution of Dürer's art towards the revival and revivification of the great tradition of Netherlandish painting, especially through his graphic work. Julius Held carried out a careful and extensive enquiry into the extent of the debt owed by the Netherlandish artists to the engravings of their great German colleague ([1]). Held confined himself, however, to looking at the works of art and discovering in each the details derived from Dürer's work. The Diary sheds a direct light on Dürer's relationship with the artists of the Low Countries.

As we have said, the journey was primarily a business undertaking. Dürer's first concern was to extend the sale and diffusion of his engravings. His luggage contained a considerable number of his "books" of wood-cuts: the Apocalypse, the "Large" Passion, the Life of the Virgin, the "Small" Passion, as well as a large number of separate plates. One may recall that Dürer was his own publisher and organised the sale of his own engravings. Earlier, the sale of his engravings was entrusted to his mother and his wife, and most probably to his pupils also. By 1520, he had executed the best part of his graphic work, which comprised some one hundred copper engravings and about two hundred wood-cuts, to which number only a very few plates were subsequently to be added.

The fact that Dürer carried with him so many "books" as well as separate plates indicates that he was confident of finding a market for them in the Netherlands. He had known for some time that his engravings were in demand in the Netherlands, where they were circulated in the workshops to be used as a repertoire of new forms, figures, themes and compositions, to which an artist could refer to his heart's content.

It is no exaggeration to say that it was through Dürer's work that Renaissance art was revealed to Netherlandish artists. Dürer gave them a host of new designs and ideas, and instructed them in the rudiments of the new style. Indeed, the Netherlandish painters of the beginning of the sixteenth century derived far more from Dürer than from the Italians. This is not very surprising when one considers

([1]) Julius HELD. – *Dürers Wirkung auf die Niederländische Kunst seiner Zeit*, The Hague, 1931.

CHAPTER III

that Dürer, in spite of his own debt to Italy, remained impregnated with the spirit of the Middle Ages and the Gothic style of painting even in his most advanced and daring experiments. Thus, to the Netherlandish artists he would appear to be a model to whom they could refer with confidence. Dürer's wood-cuts made a far greater impression in the Netherlands than did the celebrated engravings by Marc Antonio Raimondi.

It is the engravings that explain Dürer's dominant influence over Netherlandish artists. Held remarked, with good reason, that at the beginning of the sixteenth century the painters were concerned above all with increasing their stock of pictorial motifs, of figures, poses and physiognomical expressions. At a time when the idea of originality and individuality was not yet current, artists would see nothing improper in taking ideas from others to enrich their own compositions. One of the *raisons d'être* of the engraving was precisely that it could serve this purpose so well: the easily transportable prints were circulated in the workshops where they provided new models and ideas. They were not copied in a slavish manner, but the purpose was to extract some specific motif.

There was no-one better able than Dürer to supply the workshops of the Netherlandish painters with this material through his graphic works, for no other painter possessed his endless invention. There is no end to the list of new themes or personal interpretations of traditional themes which he introduced into his series of engravings and separate plates. Never before had the world seen such abundant creativity nor known so prolific a fantasy, always based upon a penetrating and exact study of reality.

Dürer's name was famous and his art well-known and admired in the Netherlands. One is not surprised to read in Dürer's Diary of the marks of esteem and admiration that he received from his Netherlandish colleagues throughout his stay. Dürer, just under fifty years of age on his arrival in the Netherlands, was welcomed everywhere like a prince, with receptions and banquets given in his honour. Artists competed with one another in their efforts to please him and to seek to be of service to him. The banquets held in Antwerp, Bruges and Ghent were lavish affairs. Dürer does not hesitate to express his proper pride and satisfaction at these flattering demonstrations of esteem. One may note with what detail he describes in his Diary, which otherwise is devoted mainly to the detailed recording of his receipts and expenses, the way in which the painters of Antwerp and Bruges escorted him home by the light of lanterns after each banquet. At Bruges, more than sixty people escorted him in this

CHAPTER III

manner.   And at Ghent, where Dürer climbed the tower of St John's and saw the wonderful city spread out at his feet, he could not avoid telling us how he was overwhelmed to reflect that it was the same city that had showered so much honour upon him.

According to the Diary, Dürer disposed of his entire stock of engravings, either selling or exchanging them for other *objets d'art* or for all manner of objects that appealed to him, or by presenting them to people who had been of help to him or with whom he desired to be on good terms.   Through the sale of his engravings he made some one hundred florins in cash.   More often than not he would approach the buyers himself, but there were also occasions where he would engage an agent. Thus, Sebald Fischer, who shortly after Dürer's arrival, bought from him a large collection of engravings for thirty florins, appears to have been one of these agents.   So, apparently, was Jan Türck, who is no doubt to be identified with the art-dealer Jacob Tierik.

In order to give some idea of the number of engravings Dürer took with him to the Netherlands, it may be mentioned that he sold on a single occasion sixteen copies of the "Small" Passion series, and on other occasions, twelve, and six copies of the same series.   He gave away as presents complete sets of his engravings to the Regent of the Netherlands, Marguerite of Austria, and to Tommaso Vincidor, the Bolognese painter, who agreed to give him in exchange the engraved works of Marc Antonio Raimondi, and to Bernhard Stecher, Lorenz Sterck, Adriaen Herbouts and the sculptor Jean Mone.

Dürer took with him in addition to his own engravings those by Hans Schäufelein, a pupil of his, and Hans Baldung Grien, who if not a pupil was definitely one of his friends.

Shortly after Dürer arrived in Antwerp a reception was given in his honour, followed by a banquet organised by the local painters. After describing the reception Dürer remarks, in a short sentence, that he had entered Master Quentin's house. He apparently did not meet Massys, since otherwise he would surely have recorded the welcome he would have received, considering that Massys was at the peak of his career in 1520 and his reputation outshone that of the other artists in Antwerp.   There is, indeed, no mention anywhere in the Diary of a meeting taking place between Dürer and Massys. There are various possible explanations for this.   It is possible that Massys was absent when Dürer called at his home, or that he was ill, but in this case Dürer would certainly have tried to see him some other time.   We are led to believe, with Max Friedländer, that Massys avoided meeting his German colleague on account of

CHAPTER III

(¹) Max J. Friedländer. - *Die altniederländische Malerei*, vol. VII, Berlin, 1929.

shyness or, more likely, from a feeling of jealousy or pride (¹). This behaviour would appear to fit the description of his character in the few accounts that have come down to us. Massys appears, also, to have deliberately kept aloof from the Corporation of Painters, in whose Guild he never accepted any office. The house visited by Dürer was situated in the Rue des Tanneurs, under the sign of "*De Simme*" ("The Ape"), and was bought by Quentin in 1519. In 1521, the artist moved to a house with garden in the Rue des Arbalétriers, which he called "Saint Quentin" and furnished to his own taste. Later he was to decorate the walls with murals in the Italian fashion. The house "*De Simme*" was apparently one of the sights of the town and Dürer would have visited it as such. The fact that the Diary is silent about Massys is all the more puzzling since Dürer was in constant contact during his stay in Antwerp with all the painter's friends, especially Joachim Patinir, who was not only a friend of Massys but also collaborated with him on his paintings. On Patinir's death, in 1524, Quentin Massys was to act as tutor to his daughters.

For a number of reasons it would have been only logical for the two painters to get together since they had so much in common, were of much the same age and each was a leader in his profession in his respective country. Like Dürer, Massys had in his youth abandoned his profession as apprentice-craftsman in his father's workshop in order to take up painting. Like Dürer, too, he was one of the first in the West to give his profession the high reputation it now held in the public eye. In addition, Massys had borrowed abundantly from Dürer's engravings, taking from him certain attitudes of figures and certain physiognomical expressions. For instance, the figure of Herod on the left wing of his large "Pietà" altarpiece, now in Antwerp Museum, was transposed from the figure of Emperor Domitian presiding at the torture of St John the Evangelist which appears in the first of the wood-cuts of Dürer's Apocalypse series (1498). Similarly, the youth standing in the foreground in the same panel reproduces in every detail the pose of one of the executioners in Dürer's engraving. Comparable borrowings may be identified in the right wing of the same altarpiece, in which there again appears Dürer's Emperor Domitian, and, among the assistants, the more or less caricatured types that Massys had clearly taken from his German colleague's engraving.

One must not, however, attach too great a significance to the correspondences, since there was no question of deliberate plagiarism; it was simply that Massys used certain elements from whatever

CHAPTER III

engravings chanced to come his way. Only rarely may one find any trace of Dürer in other works by Massys. Massys' special contribution to Netherlandish painting resides in his facial types and expressions and in the depiction of ugliness, which, if at times it may owe something to his German contemporary, was inspired from a very different source. It was the caricatures by Leonardo da Vinci that appear to have set Massys on this path, both realistic and expressive, of which typical examples are the profile portrait of a man in the Jacquemart-André Museum in Paris and the "Monstrous Woman" in the Blaker Collection in London.

Was it perhaps in Quentin's house that Dürer saw some work by the Netherlandish master which impressed him so much that he wanted to do the same? That is, a painting of "Saint Jerome in his study", now lost but believed to be the prototype of the many "Saint Jeromes" produced by Massys' followers: by his son Jan, and by Marinus van Roymerswaele, Joos van Cleef and Jan Sanders van Hemessen. Until some evidence is found, it is impossible to say whether the priority for the composition of the half-length "Saint Jerome" meditating in front of a skull with books scattered on the table belongs to Dürer or Massys. In any event, it was in Antwerp that Dürer painted his "Saint Jerome" now in Lisbon Museum([1]). It is also an interesting circumstance that Saint Jerome had become a sort of patron saint of painters of landscape, genre and still-life in Antwerp.

The Diary helps us to reconstruct the various stages of Dürer's famous painting of Saint Jerome. As early as October 1520, when passing through Cologne, Dürer acquired a skull, which he was later to place in the foreground of his composition : "I paid 2 white pf. for a little skull", he writes in his Diary.

A few months later, in January 1521, when back in Antwerp, he writes : "I gave 3 st. to the man whose portrait I drew". This was probably the old man who sat for the study for the Saint now in the Albertina in Vienna. Dürer wrote about his model as follows : *"Der man was alt 93 jor vnd noch gesund vnd fermuglich zw antorff"* (The man was 93 years of age and was in good health and living comfortably here in Antwerp). The figure of Saint Jerome in the painting was based on this study. Towards the end of March of the same year Dürer refers in his Diary to the painting : "I have painted a Jerome carefully in oils and gave it to Rodrigo of Portugal". He had made a number of preliminary drawings for the painting in black-and-white on grey paper, including a study of a hand, a study for the skull and a study for the book-rest. The Diary states further that Dürer exchanged the old frame of the "Saint Jerome"

CHAPTER III

(1) See Plate I, p. 25 and Plates 43 and 47.

for another frame intended for a portrait (1). Rodrigo took the painting back with him to Portugal where it is to-day.

Whether or not the painting was inspired by one of Massys' works, it certainly exercised a great influence on the Antwerp painters, who were later to try to emulate Dürer's interpretation of the theme. The success of the painting no doubt depended on its considerable artistic merit — and we know the great pains Dürer took with the painting — but it was due also to the fact that it reflected so well the spirit of the times with its aspirations towards religious reform. The old man in the painting who looks out at the spectator with insistent gaze, pointing a finger in no less imperative a manner at the skull before him, is clearly intended to remind Christians of their mortal state and exhort them to dwell on their ultimate end. In an age when disorder and frivolous thinking were rife in many a religious establishment, a painting such as this could be conceived by the pious Dürer as a summons to return to the essential truths of the faith. Its effect was thus comparable to that of Luther's sermons and writings.

Having said this, it is not surprising to find that, after Dürer, the painter who was to work on the same subject time and again was Marinus van Roymerswaele, a keen supporter of the Reformation. In his painting of Saint Jerome, Marinus was able to achieve an even more arresting facial expression by giving the Saint the features of an emaciated old man, whose skeleton-like hands, with long, gnarled fingers and large protruding veins, and whose terrifying mask-like face give the impression of a fearful apparition. One of the few facts known about this painter explains his strange obsessional nature. In 1566 van Roymerswaele was in Middelburg where he was condemned for taking part in the iconoclastic disturbances — that is, the painter was an accomplice in the destruction of works of art that offended his religious conscience.

Another prominent Netherlandish painter at the time was Joos van Cleef. He, too, was working on a version of the same subject when Dürer was still in Antwerp. Among all the painters of Antwerp he followed most faithfully the composition of the Lisbon painting. In contrast to Roymerswaele, he modified the painting in the direction of giving a softer and less disturbing expression to the Saint. Van Cleef was clearly more concerned with harmony of form than with religious conversion. He also employed motifs from Dürer's engravings in his other works. In his "Pietà" in the Louvre Museum he adopts the same pose for the Virgin collapsed on the ground as that in Dürer's wood-cut of "Christ taking leave of His Mother" (2). And again, van Cleef's panel of the Reinhold altarpiece in Danzig

(2) Julius HELD. - *Op. cit.*

CHAPTER III

is a free copy after the "Ecce Homo" of Dürer's wood-cut series of the "Small" Passion of 1511. It is surprising that Dürer does not mention van Cleef in his Diary, who in 1520 lived close to the Chapelle des Grâces in Antwerp. Like Massys, van Cleef was a close friend of Patinir and it is almost certain that the two painters collaborated together.

The Diary is less silent about Patinir. Almost immediately after Dürer arrived in Antwerp he got in touch with Patinir. The two painters appear to have got on well, and they often dined together and exchanged ideas. Patinir lent Dürer his apprentice and also his colours. In return Dürer presented the master and apprentice with some of his engravings.

Later, Master Adrian, that is Adriaen Herbouts, Secretary to the town of Antwerp and a friend of the Humanists, was to give Dürer a small panel painting by Patinir of "Lot and his Daughters". Patinir invited Dürer to his wedding, which took place on the Sunday before Ascension, and treated him as a guest of honour. Before leaving Antwerp Dürer presented Patinir with a few engravings by the German painter Hans Baldung Grien.

In his Diary Dürer calls Patinir : "the good landscape painter". We know that the artist specialised in painting panoramic landscapes, in which fantasy and reality were blended to perfection. Patinir added the backgrounds to many works by Massys and van Cleef (one painting at least, the "Temptation of Saint Anthony" in the Prado Museum, is known to be a work of collaboration between Patinir and Massys). As a typical specialist Patinir showed great skill in his own particular field but was less successful when he essayed other types of work. The drawing of the human figure was not his forte, and Dürer was to come to his aid by making four drawings of Saint Christopher on a brown-toned paper. It is possible that Patinir used one of these studies for his large "Saint Christopher" which occupies the central position in his Escorial painting. Panofsky points out the connection between this figure and the same figure in reverse in Dürer's engraving of the same subject, both works executed in 1521.

Earlier, Dürer had drawn in metal-point *"ein Angesicht"* (a face) which was clearly intended for a figure in some landscape by Patinir. At the same time Dürer also made his colleague's portrait — the drawing is no longer known, but is almost certainly recorded in an engraving made by Cornelis Cort de Hoorn in 1572 for the Lampsonius Collection, in which the Antwerp artist appears to be something over fifty years of age.

CHAPTER III

Carel van Mander records the relationship between Patinir and Dürer in the Netherlands, basing his information on the engraving by Cort and the verse beneath the portrait written by Lampsonius :

Maer om dat Dürer sagh Landtschappen, putten, rotsen,
Van u geschildert cloeck, verwondert zynde seer,
Met Coper stift op ley u wesen track wel eer.

This tells us that Dürer made Patinir's portrait with the copperpoint. He adds that the Antwerp painter led a somewhat irregular life, and would spend whole days in the tavern drinking his money away, for he was a heavy drinker and when there was nothing left he would need to fall back upon "his lucrative brushes".

At the end of August 1520 Dürer went to Brussels. He was particularly struck by the beauty of the city and praised especially the Town Hall, the "gardens of Paradise" of the Palace of the Dukes of Brabant and, above all, the objects of gold and silver, the strange armour and exotic costumes sent to the King of Spain from America. It is likely that while he was in Brussels Dürer tried to establish good relations with certain officials in Marguerite of Austria's Court. After meeting Konrad Meit, sculptor to the Regent Marguerite, he made the acquaintance of her painter, Bernard van Orley. The latter invited him to a lavish dinner party which made an enormous impression upon him, prompting him to write "I do not think 10 fl. will pay for it". He met a few well-known people at the dinner whom he says had invited themselves to pay him homage. They included the Marshal of the Court, Jean de Metenye, the Town Treasurer, Gilles of Busleyden, and finally the Treasurer to the Regent, Don Diego Flores, whose portrait he painted.

The first time Dürer met van Orley was when the latter was completing his "Job" altarpiece, which is dated in 1521 (Brussels Museum). The painter was in his late twenties and had been held in high esteem at the Court for some five years. He had been appointed titular painter to Marguerite of Austria, a position previously filled by Jacopo de'Barbari, the "Master of the Caduceus", the Venetian painter whose "little book" Dürer admired so much when it was shown to him by the Regent in her collection at Malines, that he begged her to give it to him. The Regent had, however, already promised the book to her painter Bernard van Orley. The "little book" no doubt contained Jacopo's studies of proportion.

It cannot be said that Dürer's work exercised any influence on Bernard van Orley, whose one aim was to emulate Raphael, whose tapestries

I. *Saint Jerome.* Museum of Fine Arts, Lisbon.

for the Sistine Chapel were being completed in Pieter van Aelst's workshop in Brussels. Nevertheless, it is probable that the example of Dürer's manifold activity in the Netherlands — the host of sketches and designs of all kinds, including portraits, coats-of-arms, decorative schemes and costume designs — stimulated Orley's inventive genius. Orley also prided himself on his ability to invent figural and decorative forms. He believed that the nobility of art resided in artistic creativity, and he left it to the craftsmen to carry out his artistic conceptions.

Some lines further on Dürer writes that he has made "the portrait in charcoal of Master Bernard, Lady Margaret's painter". It is not known whether the portrait still exists. Some writers, like Eduard Flechsig [1], are tempted to identify it with the portrait of a young man in front-view now at the Bonnat Museum in Bayonne, dated 1520, which certainly bears some resemblance to Orley as he appears in the engraving in the Lampsonius Collection.

It had been supposed that Dürer also made a portrait of Orley in oils from the entry in the Diary which reads: "I painted Bernhard von Resten's portrait in oils, for which he paid me 8 fl., and gave my wife a crown, and Susanna a florin worth 24 st.". Both manuscripts of the Diary clearly read: "Bernhard von Resten". In their edition of the Diary, Lange and Fuhse substituted the word "Bresslen" for "Resten", but there is nothing to support this reading. Sometime later, Henri Hymans, who based his edition on Lange and Fuhse's, considered the "Bresslen" to refer to "Brussels", but again without any foundation, since Dürer always used the word "Prussel" for "Brussels". It was then easy to take the next step and decide that "Bernhard of Brussels" could be no other than Bernard van Orley.

The portrait in question has been identified with that in the Dresden Museum (No. 1871), painted against a red ground. The person in the painting holds a letter in his left hand which reads: "Dem pernh... zw...". Since it is dated in 1521 and is painted on an oak panel it was most probably executed in the Netherlands. Everything points to the probability of this being the portrait referred to in the Diary but there is nothing that allows us to conclude that the sitter was Bernard van Orley and not Bernhard von Resten whose name is clearly written in both the manuscripts.

Furthermore, the Diary tells us that the portrait was done in Antwerp, and van Orley lived in Brussels. Dürer did not say that a painter had posed for him, whereas he makes a point of saying so in the case of the portrait he made in charcoal of van Orley, and he never fails to write "Master" before the name of painters mentioned in his Diary. It is, therefore, preferable to believe, with Eduard Flechsig, that the

[1] Eduard FLECHSIG. - *Albrecht Dürer*, Berlin, 1928-1931.

CHAPTER III

27

portrait in Dresden represents a man named Bernhard von Resten, probably a German merchant, who lived in Antwerp.

It may also be pointed out that the name Bernard appears on two other occasions in the Diary when it could not possibly refer to van Orley. In December 1520, Dürer painted the portraits of "little Bernard of Bresslen, Georg Kötzler and the Frenchman from Kamrich" in Bergen-op-Zoom. The word "little" would hardly make sense if van Orley were intended. An in 1521, when still in Antwerp, Dürer made a drawing in charcoal of a Bernhard von Castel from whom he had won some money at gambling.

Dürer's relationship with Jan Prevost is important in so far as it serves to emphasise the close connections that existed at the time between the School of Bruges and that of Antwerp. The growing prosperity of Antwerp attracted the painters of Bruges to transfer their workshops to Antwerp, or at least to work in the city for a time. There is every reason to believe that Patinir and Joos van Cleef passed their apprenticeship in Bruges and that they settled soon afterwards in the young cosmopolitan city. We know that Gerard David lived in Antwerp in 1515.

Jan Prevost, a native of Mons, had been living in Bruges for some twenty-five years, but it was in Antwerp, in the autumn of 1520, that Dürer was to meet him. Dürer made his portrait in charcoal for which Prevost gave him a florin. Dürer on that occasion refers to him as : "*De Meister Jan Prost von Pruck*".

In the spring of the following year Prevost was again in Antwerp, and this time he returned to Bruges in the company of Dürer and a certain Hans Lieber of Ulm. The Diary reads : "*Jan Prevost, ein guter Maler von Prug burtig*". This information is, however, inaccurate.

Prevost invited Dürer to stay at his house in Bruges and on the evening of their arrival gave a dinner in his honour. Prevost who had been nominated Dean of the Guild of Bruges in 1519 was in the happy position of being able to do the city's honours. Dürer was received by the painters of Bruges in their quarters and offered a magnificent banquet, at the conclusion of which he was escorted home by the light of lanterns. Before leaving Bruges, he made another drawing of Prevost in metal-point. By way of a parting gift Dürer gave ten deniers to his host's wife.

Like many other painters from the Netherlands, Prevost had already known Dürer's work through his engravings. In his painting of "Saint Catherine disputing with the Doctors" (Boymans Museum, Rotterdam) he had used the face of Dürer's Emperor Domitian in the same way that Massys had done.

CHAPTER III

It is a pity that Dürer does not mention any other painter from Bruges, for it is clear that many were influenced by him. There was, for example, the anonymous painter who, although known as the "Bruges Master of 1500", it would be more appropriate to call "The Master of 1515". This eclectic painter, who imitated the work of such painters as the Master of Flémalle, Memlinc and Dürer, had taken his "Cruxifixion" in the Church of Saint Saviour (1511) from Dürer's wood-cut of the "Large" Passion.

It was towards the end of his stay in Antwerp, on the 10th of June 1521, that Dürer got in touch with an artist in the Netherlands for whom he had the greatest admiration and in whom he was particularly interested, that is, Lukas van Leyden. This artist was also both painter and engraver and his engravings were enjoying a popular success at the time. The Diary contains the simple sentence : "Master Lukas who engraves in copper asked me as his guest. He is a little man, born at Leyden in Holland; he was at Antwerp". Two days later, Dürer records that he has drawn "with the metal-point" the portrait of Master Lukas of Leyden. Further on he writes "I gave 8 fl. worth of my prints for a whole set of Lukas' engravings", from which we may deduce that the two artists were on very good terms and that they were pleased to have each other's engravings.

Carel van Mander embroiders the terse and somewhat dry statement of Dürer's Diary and gives a more picturesque if plausible account of the relationship between the two artists. He describes the first meeting between them in this manner : "When Dürer saw Lukas van Leyden he seems to have been taken aback by his appearance and was moved to such an extent that he was left breathless and his speech failed him. He then took him affectionately by the arm and wondered at the contrast between the man's small stature and his great and glorious name." For his part, Lukas took particular pleasure in contemplating his elder colleague, whose engravings he had known for some time and whose fame had already reached him. These two "lights and ornaments", the one from Germany and the other from the Low Countries, made each other's portraits and enjoyed greatly each other's company. Van Mander goes on to say, but in a less sure manner : "Some believe that Albrecht Dürer and he tended to be suspicious of each other, that is, that they tried to rival each other, and that on occasions Lukas would make an engraving of the same subject as Dürer, whatever it might be and without any hesitation, yet the two artists were to admire their mutual achievements to such an extent that Dürer made a journey to the Low Countries and during his stay in Leyden with Lukas he painted his portrait from life on a

CHAPTER III

29

small panel, and they remained on good terms with one another." Carel van Mander's account is true, except in so far as it places the meeting between the two artists in Leyden. It is an undeniable fact that Lukas was inspired by a spirit of rivalry. In particular, it was Dürer's example that encouraged the Dutch painter to make his large drawings of heads under the guise of portraits, almost all of which were made during Lukas's brief stay in Antwerp. Indeed, the artist's individuality was soon to assert itself again very definitely and he was in no way to become a servile follower of his elder master. He was to give an original and individual character to his bust-length portrait drawings, horizontal in format (influence of Konrad Meit's carved busts?), whereas all the portrait drawings made by Dürer in the Netherlands are upright in format. One may also detect in Lukas van Leyden a concern with style, in his use of long hatched strokes to achieve linear effects, which does not appear to have been a special concern of Dürer's. There is, however, a striking similarity otherwise between the two groups of portraits [1].

[1] Max J. FRIEDLÄNDER. - *Die altniederländische Malerei*, vol. X, Berlin, 1932.

As far as the portraits mentioned by van Mander are concerned, Dürer's Diary does support in part the remarks made by the old historian of Netherlandish art. If we know nothing about the painted portrait, Dürer's drawing of Lukas still exists (Musée Wicar, Lille). The identity of the model is well established. The resemblance to Lukas in his own self-portrait is not too obvious, but this can be readily explained by the difference in date of the two portraits : Lukas was twenty-seven years of age when he met Dürer, but only a very precocious fifteen to eighteen years of age when he made the self-portrait in Brunswick Museum. Furthermore, it was after the drawing in Lille that the engraving in the Lampsonius Collection was made in 1572, and this would appear to be sufficient proof of the sitter's identity. Dürer shows his colleague as an ailing man, afflicted by the tuberculosis from which he was to die some years later.

It is not only Lukas van Leyden's portrait drawings that recall Dürer. Julius Held has demonstrated that Lukas's engravings begin to betray Dürer's influence precisely from the time of his meeting with the great German artist. His copper-engraving of the Passion, dated in 1521, depends directly on a number of Dürer's compositions. Van Mander's statement that Lukas was so disturbed by Dürer's success that he sought to emulate him in all things to prove himself an equal was probably not an exaggeration.

The contact between the two masters could not have lasted long, since on the 28th of June, exactly two weeks after Dürer had drawn his portrait, Lukas returned to Leyden where he stood surety for his

CHAPTER III

brother. Some years later he was to return to the Southern States on a tour through Zeeland, Brabant and Flanders, following very much the itinerary of Dürer's journey, in order to market his engravings.

At the time of Dürer's stay in Antwerp, there was an artist there who knew better than Massys or van Orley how to give shape to the new aspirations in Netherlandish art. This was Dirck Vellert, a painter as well as a designer for painting on glass, whose work covered a wide range of interests. Vellert followed in the footsteps of Dürer and the Italian Renaissance masters in his use of a variety of techniques. As a designer for painting on glass he not only made the designs, as Massys and van Orley had done, but also executed the painting on the glass. It was Guichardin who records this information, which is supported by the few lines that Dürer devotes to Vellert. We may in the first place observe how Dürer refers to Vellert on every occasion as both painter and glass-painter. Furthermore, the first time Dürer mentions the artist, he notes that "Master Dierick sent me the red colour that is found at Antwerp in the new bricks". What colour did he mean exactly? Was it a pigment which, mixed with oil or the white of an egg, would be a suitable medium for panel painting? Or was it something used specifically by glass-painters? Hermann Schmitz believed in the latter possibility, and he drew Veth and Müller's attention (¹) to the fact that Dürer himself bought on a number of occasions some of the colour "which is found in bricks" after he had tried the sample given him by Vellert. Soon after Dürer's return to Nuremberg, a certain red colour, which had already appeared in Antwerp painted glass, was being used by German panel painters and glass-painters. It is possible that the stock which Dürer took back with him was intended for his German colleagues.

(¹) J. VETH and S. MÜLLER. – *Albrecht Dürers Niederländische Reise*, Berlin, 1918.

Dirck Vellert who, as a typical eclectic artist, borrowed ideas for his engravings and designs from Lukas van Leyden, and from Mantegna and many other Italian painters, was a great admirer of Dürer and used his engravings on more than one occasion. "I gave Master Dietrich the glass-painter an *Apocalypse* and the *6 Knots*", Dürer writes at the beginning of 1521. The gift was not lost on the Antwerp painter, who reciprocated by presenting Dürer with an Apocalypse of his own which closely followed Dürer's print; and in 1532, he produced a series of engravings of the Life of the Virgin which again made use of many elements from Dürer's compositions. Vellert is next mentioned in the Diary in May 1521, when Dürer declares him to be one of the most prosperous and highly esteemed

CHAPTER III   31 artists of his time : on the Sunday after Ascension Dirck gave a dinner to which Dürer and other high-ranking people were invited : "We had a costly feast, and they did me a great honour", writes Dürer.

Dürer was to meet many other glass-painters in Antwerp, where the genre was especially favoured. Stained or painted glass was not restricted to the adornment of churches, but also took its part in the decoration of palaces and houses. Small roundels or medallions painted in grisaille heightened in silver-yellow were particularly in demand. Vellert was a specialist in the art of painting such "cabinet windows", and so also was another Antwerp painter, Aert van Ort, known as "Ortkens", also mentioned by Dürer in his Diary : "I gave Master Aert, the glasspainter, a *Life of Our Lady*." [1] It goes without saying that such a gift must have offered Ortkens a new source of ideas for his painted glass medallions.

Dürer mentions two other glass-painters to whom he gave similar assistance : a certain Hönigin, to whom he gave two large books, and one of Vellert's students by the name of Henne Doghens, about whom Dürer writes : "I gave glazier Hennik's son 2 Books".

These few examples help to indicate the extent of the influence exercised by Dürer's wood-cuts on the art of glass-painting in Antwerp.

We learn from the Diary that Dürer kept in contact with two sculptors : the German Konrad Meit and Jean Mone from Lorraine. Dürer shows a special respect for the first, who lived in Malines and was in the service of Marguerite of Austria. It appears that Dürer had already met him some years previously, probably at Wittenberg at the court of the Elector of Saxony, where Meit, a native of Worms, had worked from about 1506 to 1509 [2]. As soon as Dürer reached Antwerp he arranged through Gilles von Apfennauwe, a German nobleman, to send the sculptor some of his engravings. In this way he no doubt hoped to find a sympathiser in Meit who might exert some pressure on Marguerite of Austria in the matter of the confirmation of his Imperial pension. Even at this point, before he actually met Meit in the Netherlands, Dürer mentions him in the following flattering terms : "... whose like I have not seen. He is in the service of Lady Margaret, the Emperor's daughter".

A few days later Dürer goes to Malines as Konrad Meit's guest, and repeats that : "Master Konrad is the good carver in Lady Margaret's service". Dürer then continued his journey to Brussels, apparently in the company of Konrad Meit who probably proposed to introduce him to the Regent. The Diary reads : "I took a portrait at night by candlelight of Master Konrad of Brussels, who was my host."

[1] Guichardin writes in praise of Ortkens, whom he calls Art van Hort di Nimega.

[2] Jos. DUVERGER. - *Conrad Meyt*, Brussels, 1934.

CHAPTER III

II. *Bernhard von Resten*. Gemäldegalerie, Dresden.

The following year, at Whitsuntide, Dürer in his turn invited the sculptor to Antwerp, and when they parted company they exchanged presents. Dürer writes : "Master Konrad gave me a fine pair of knives, so I gave his little old man a *Life of Our Lady* in return." In the absence of any evidence to prove that Meit had any pupils, we may assume that the "little old man" was simply a "servant". Finally, in June of the same year, a few weeks before his departure, Dürer was again to visit Malines, when he invited Konrad to his place on two occasions and his wife on one occasion, and made a further portrait of his friend in charcoal.

Despite their friendly relationship, the frequent meetings of the two artists and the great admiration Dürer professes for Meit, he never once mentions his sculptures. We may be properly surprised at this omission, especially since Meit received his artistic training in Germany and had more than once borrowed ideas from Dürer's engravings. His "Adam and Eve" in the Gotha Museum was transposed from Dürer's wood-cut of the same subject.

Jean Mone, a sculptor originally from Metz, was living in Antwerp at the time of Dürer's visit. In 1524 he was to settle in Malines at the request of the Magistracy of the Town who granted him an annual pension. At the beginning of 1521 Dürer writes : "I took a portrait in black chalk of the good marble sculptor Master Jean, who is like Christoph Coler. He has studied in Italy and comes from Metz." This must be the sculptor Jean Mone, who we know was born in Thionville or Metz, and was the author of the carved tombs of Arnoul de Hornes in Anderlecht [1] and of Cardinal Guillaume de Croy in Héverlé.

Dürer befriended this artist too, and gave him a whole collection of his engravings before leaving the Netherlands; Jean Mone on his part making a present of six little flasks of rose-water for Dürer's wife : "very finely made", comments Dürer. It may be an appropriate place to point out that, whilst almost every line of the Diary provides us with invaluable information about a host of people and events, it is necessary to be very circumspect in the interpretation of the text, and to consider carefully each word in order to avoid arriving at false or misleading conclusions. Thus, Paul Saintenoy translated the words "*sind gar köstlich gemacht*" [2], referring to the flasks of rose-water, as : "they are very costly", and concluded on this evidence that Jean Mone was extremely prosperous in Antwerp and lived a life of more than ordinary ease. Nothing in the Diary supports any such conclusion.

As in the case of Konrad Meit, it would be easy to point out connections

[1] D. ROGGEN. - *De Beeldhouwer Jan Mone. (Communication au Congrès d'Histoire de l'Art à Bruxelles*, 1930.)

[2] Paul SAINTENOY. - *Jehan Money*, Brussels, 1931.

between the work of Jean Mone and that of Dürer. In particular, the votive sculpture in bas-relief representing the Enthroned Virgin, in Gresbeck, is inspired by the decorative motifs in Dürer's ambitious decorative schemes for the Triumph of Emperor Maximilian of 1522.

CHAPTER III

ALTHOUGH THE REFERENCES IN THE DIARY TO
the works of art seen and admired by Dürer in the Netherlands are
very brief, they are of immense value for the purpose of identifying
paintings about which no other record exists, and for providing information about lost works by famous artists.

Thus, a passage in the Diary concerning Dürer's visit to Cologne
brings to light the painter Stefan Lochner whose famous "Adoration
of the Magi", now in Cologne Cathedral, was at the time in the old
Town Hall : "I paid 2 white pf. for opening the picture at Köln
which Master Stefan made", is Dürer's brief entry.

During his first visit to Brussels Dürer visited the Town Hall where
he admired the four pictures in the "Golden Room" by the great
master Roger van der Weyden. These are certainly the important
series of paintings representing Justice made by the master shortly
before his appointment as Painter to the Town of Brussels in 1436.
Both Dirk Bouts, in his "Judgment of Otto", painted for the
Town Hall of Louvain, and Gerard David, in his "Judgment of
Cambises", painted for the Town Hall of Bruges, followed Roger's
paintings.

Two of Roger van der Weyden's panels were devoted to the Judgment
of the Emperor Trajan, and the other two represented the Judgment
of Archambault. They were destroyed in 1695 during the bom-
bardment of Brussels by the French Marshal Villeroy, but are recorded
in the tapestries woven during Roger's lifetime and now in Berne
Museum.

There is every reason to believe that the four paintings of the Judgment
were executed around 1435. The fact that van der Weyden invested
large sums of money in life annuities on the 20th October of that
year indicates that he had substantial funds in hand at the time.
Furthermore, on the 2nd May 1436 the Magistracy of Brussels
decreed : "that after the death of Master Roger there shall be no
successor to his post of Town Painter". This declaration would
hardly have been made unless such a stipulation had already been
made in Roger's contract as Town Painter. Hulin de Loo supports
this view when he declares that it was the Town's intention not to
make a precedent of Roger's nomination. The same scholar recalls
that in 1456 another German traveller, in his "Mystic Contemplation",
had already praised the excellence of the paintings; and later, Guichardin, Vasari and Molanus were all to make eulogistic comments on
the works.

Dürer had the opportunity to see yet another important work
by Roger van der Weyden in Brussels, since the remark that he

CHAPTER IV

paid "2 st. for opening St Luke's picture" can only refer to the painting by Roger now lost but recorded in a number of copies probably made in the master's own workshop, the best of which are now in the Museum of Fine Arts in Boston and in the Munich Pinacoteca. The altarpiece seen by Dürer was probably at the time in the painters' chapel. Roger's treatment of the painting was remarkably similar to Jan van Eyck's : the landscape, with the river extending as far as the eye can see, and the two figures, their elbows resting on the parapet at the bend of the road, clearly depend on the background of van Eyck's "Madonna of Chancellor Rolin". This allows us to place the date of the painting somewhere between 1435 and 1440 when van der Weyden was in the service of the Burgundian Court and was associated with Chancellor Rolin who was later to commission the artist to paint the "Last Judgment" for the hospital in Beaune.

After admiring the Altarpiece of Saint Luke, Dürer went to see, also in Brussels, "the good picture that Master Hugo painted" in the chapel of the House of the Counts of Nassau. Master Hugo is of course Hugo van der Goes, who was apparently still held in very high esteem, to judge from the respect with which Dürer always mentions his name. It had been thought that the Altarpiece in question represented the Seven Sacraments, but it is quite impossible to make any definite pronouncement.

If Dürer no more than mentions Quentin Massys by name, he also does not appear to have met Jan Gossaert, who was after Massys the most highly esteemed Netherlandish painter of the time. Dürer did indeed see one of the artist's greatest paintings, the triptych that adorned the High Altar of the Premonstratensian Abbey in Middelburg, which according to Carel van Mander was so big and heavy that the wings required supports to hold them open. The Altarpiece, which had as a central panel a painting representing the Crucifixion, had only just been erected. It had been commissioned by the Abbot Maximilian of Burgundy, a son of Baudouin and nephew of Gossaert's patron the illegitimate Philip of Burgundy. The painting was destroyed by fire in the Church in 1568.

It was the type of painting to excite Dürer's special interest. Gossaert approached Dürer in his style of painting more closely than did any other Netherlandish painter. In the past, he had borrowed very much from Dürer's engravings. His large painting of "Neptune and Amphitrite" clearly derives from Dürer's engraving of "Adam and Eve" of 1504; and the little dog placed in the foreground of the large painting of the "Adoration of the Magi" in the National Gallery is copied quite literally from one of the dogs in the engraving of "Saint Eustace" by the German master.

It is strange that it should have been this Triptych in Middelburg that prompted Dürer to pass the one criticism he ever made of the works of his Netherlandish colleagues, when he remarks : "There, in the Abbey, is a great picture painted by Jan de Mabuse, not so good in the modelling as in the colouring". From what we know of Gossaert's art, Dürer's remark was quite pertinent.

Dürer's comment shows that he recognised the defects and merits that we now see as characteristic not only of certain works by Gossaert but of painting in general in the Low Countries at this time. The painters, in their desire to break with the more reflective and static art of the early masters and to introduce in its place a more complex and vital art, often only succeeded in producing paintings lacking in unity or balance, and full of superficial agitation and exaggerated poses, gestures and foreshortenings. Their technique alone remained exemplary and continued the great tradition of the masters of the fifteenth century. Apparently, the Middelburg Triptych presented just that combination of technical skill and weaknesses, and Dürer's comment shows a remarkable discernment.

During his stay in Bruges, where as we know he was the guest of his colleague Jan Prevost, he was shown works of art by the great masters of the preceding century. Dürer remembers three of them, and it is always the same three he writes about : Jan van Eyck, Roger van der Weyden and Hugo van der Goes. He had already made the acquaintance of the last two during his visit to Brussels. It is remarkable that he never mentions the name of Memlinc, nor the names of Hubert van Eyck or Dirk Bouts. However, we probably cannot draw any conclusions from his silence, since it seems that he also omitted to record other important events. Nevertheless, it is clear that the most famous names among the great Netherlandish masters of the past century were precisely those of Jan van Eyck, Roger van der Weyden and Hugo van der Goes. Dürer writes that he had seen "the chapel there which Roger painted" which was in the old Imperial Palace, that is, in the Palace of the Dukes of Burgundy in Bruges. The word "chapel" is a little ambiguous. No-one has suggested that it refers to a carved altarpiece with wings painted by Roger. It is, however, very likely that it refers to the mural decorations that adorned the oratory in the Palace. The Italian Humanist Bartolomeus Facius, in his "*De Virus Illustribus*", which dedicates a notice to Roger van der Weyden, tells us that the artist painted in Brussels an "*aedes sacra*". "In Brussels", writes Facius, "which

CHAPTER IV

is a town of Gaul, he painted a holy edifice perfect in workmanship."
Furthermore, Hulin de Loo, after quoting this passage, records that
a long time ago, during the demolition of a vault in Louvain, some
paintings of angels were uncovered, similar in style to Roger's.
It may well be that it was just such a wall-painting that Dürer saw in
the Emperor's Palace.

"They took me next to S. Jacob's", Dürer writes, "and showed me
the precious pictures by Roger and Hugo, who were both great
masters." Carel van Mander confirmed the existence of a painting
by Hugo van der Goes in the Church of Saint James. He describes
it as a painting of the Crucifixion, with the thieves, the Virgin and
other figures. Sanderus and Descamps, on the other hand, talk
of a painting by the same artist in the High Altar of the church
representing the Descent from the Cross. This latter identification
appears to be nearer the truth. Indeed, we know that many copies
were made of Hugo van der Goes' "Pietà", showing the figures in
half-length (Ghent Museum, Tournai Museum, the Jesuit Convent in
Ghent, etc.). Few compositions have enjoyed such popularity,
and the numerous copies lead one to suppose that the painting was
exhibited in some public place. It is for this reason that Friedländer
believed that the painting seen by Dürer was the one originally in
the High Altar of Saint James church and now lost. As far as van der

(¹) James WEALE. - Bruges et
ses environs, Bruges, 1862.

Weyden is concerned, James Weale has pointed out (¹) that in 1476
a certain Battista de Aquelli, a Pisan merchant, founded an altarpiece
in the church of Saint James in Bruges, which was painted by Roger
and represented the life of Saint John the Baptist. It is probable
that this altarpiece, a copy of which is in Berlin, was one of the paintings
admired by Dürer in the church of Saint James.

The fact that Dürer saw several works of art by Roger van der Weyden
in Bruges is not without significance. It offers additional evidence
to such writers as Emile Renders, who believe that van der Weyden
lived for some time in that town and was a pupil of Jan van Eyck.
One may also recall that Carel van Mander refers to a "Roger van
Brugghe" as one of van Eyck's pupils. Later, van Vaernewijck,
an archaeologist from Ghent, confirms, in his book "*Historie van
Belgis*" (1568), the existence of many works by Roger in Bruges :
"*Die stadt van Brugghe is verschiert niet alleene in die kercken maer ook
in die huysen van... meester Rogiers... schilderie.*" (The town of Bruges
is full of paintings by Master Roger not only in churches but also
in the houses.)

Dürer also saw Michelangelo's Virgin and Child "in alabaster" in
the Cathedral in Bruges, where it remains to-day.

CHAPTER IV

He also visited other churches and the painters' chapel in Bruges, remarking upon the countless fine things he saw but mentioning only the name of van Eyck.

It was the same in Ghent, when Dürer visited the town a few days later and was taken round by the Dean and Jurymen of the Painters' Guild. He saw, in the church of Saint John, Jan van Eyck's famous altarpiece of the Adoration of the Lamb, and writes enthusiastically: "Then I saw Jan's picture; it is a most precious painting, full of thought, and the Eve, Mary and God the Father are specially good". We may observe that Dürer refers to the central figure as the image of God the Father, whereas most modern scholars consider that the figure to whom John the Baptist points with a finger is that of Christ.

The words "Jan's picture" ("*des Johannes Tafel*") have been variously interpreted, and its meaning has an important bearing on the question of Hubert van Eyck's collaboration on the altarpiece. James Weale interprets the phrase as "the altarpiece of Saint John the Evangelist", the subject being drawn from the Apocalypse. This would not appear to be very probable, however. If it were the case, Dürer would have written something like : "*die Johannes Tafel*", ("the Saint John's Altarpiece"). The definite article is in the genitive case and would seem to apply to the author of the painting; and if this is so, it can refer only to Jan van Eyck and ignores any part Hubert van Eyck may have had in the conception and execution of the work. Friedländer and Emile Renders quoted Dürer in support of their argument against any collaboration by Hubert. Hulin de Loo put yet a third interpretation on the words "*des Johannes Tafel*", believing that Dürer was referring to "the Altarpiece of the Church of Saint John", in the same way that he had referred to the "Tower of Saint John's" a few lines earlier. This interpretation is, however, difficult to accept. Indeed, whenever Dürer refers to some specific artist's work, he writes exactly in this way, and the words seem to point well and truly to Jan van Eyck as the author of the altarpiece. Nevertheless, the words do not provide any real evidence in support of Emile Renders' thesis that even denies Hubert van Eyck's existence as an artist.

We have already referred to Dürer's visit to the Regent, Marguerite of Austria, just before he left the Netherlands. She received him in her Palace in Malines, where she showed him her collection of works of art and her library. Dürer was particularly impressed by forty small panels painted in oils : "The like of which for precision and excellence I have never beheld", he says. Evidently, the panels were those painted by Juan de Flandes for Isabel the Catholic, representing the Passion of Christ. The series consisted originally of forty-six paintings. Later, Marguerite of Austria bought back nearly all the paintings through her Treasurer, Don Diego Flores. Until recently fifteen of these exquisitely finished works formed part of the Spanish Royal collection. Others are now lost or are dispersed in the Louvre, the Albertina and Berlin.

Dürer tells us that he again saw paintings by "Jan" in the Palace in Malines. Here, once again, he refers to Jan van Eyck. From the inventory of Marguerite of Austria's collection, dated in 1515, we learn that she owned the painting of the "Virgin at the Fountain", now in Antwerp Museum, and a large picture called "Hernoul le Fin with his wife standing in a room...", undoubtedly referring to the portrait of Arnolfini and his wife in the National Gallery.

Finally, Dürer mentions another painter whom he held in high esteem and whose works of art he had seen in Marguerite of Austria's collection : "Jacob Walch", or "Jacob the Italian". This is none other than Jacopo de 'Barbari whom Dürer had met in Venice on his first visit to Italy. Jacopo had also lived for a time in Nuremberg as painter to Emperor Maximilian before entering the service of Philip of Burgundy and Marguerite of Austria. Jacopo de 'Barbari was the author of the "little book" that Dürer asked for in vain from the Regent Marguerite.

CHAPTER IV

AS PREVIOUSLY STATED, ALBRECHT DÜRER WORK-ed intensely throughout his stay in the Netherlands, even if a large part of his time was necessarily spent in travelling, in attending receptions and in his many other commitments. The Diary tells us clearly of his incessant activity. We see the artist constantly engaged in making drawings and designs of all kinds for his numerous clients : designing furniture for the German gentry, drawing plans for a house to be built for some official in Marguerite's service, designing costumes for masques, drawing figures of saints for his painter colleagues, etc. He was engaged above all, however, in the production of an immense quantity of portraits. It would seem that almost every person he met sat for him. The Diary mentions some one hundred and forty drawings, of which the greater number were portraits, and it is quite likely that there were many that he did not mention. Nearly all the portraits are large-scale charcoal drawings (approximately 35 × 25 cm.), which Dürer would normally sell to the sitter for one florin. Very many have been preserved, and attempts have been made to identify them with the help of the Diary, but this has presented problems. Up to date, the only portraits identified have been those bearing inscriptions in Dürer's hand or of which engravings were subsequently made. Some portraits drawn with the brush and others heightened in white chalk have also been preserved.

Eduard Flechsig concludes on the basis of the Diary that Dürer com-pleted eleven paintings in oils during his visit to the Netherlands, of which five were portraits. Three of the latter have been preserved: a portrait of a man in the Prado Museum, possibly representing Dürer's host in Antwerp, Jobst Plankfelt; the portrait believed to represent Bernhard von Resten in Dresden Museum; and the portrait of Lorenz Sterck in the Isabella Stewart Gardner Museum, Boston.

In addition to individual drawings and designs, Dürer executed numerous sketches, filling up many sketchbooks. We know of the existence of at least two sketchbooks used by Dürer on his travels, in which he recorded anything that attracted his attention: monuments, places, costumes, animals, etc. The first sketchbook, which he began to use on his journey by boat to Cologne, was of small size. The sheets were upright in format and the drawings were made with the pen. Some ten pages from this sketchbook are known, now widely dispersed. The portraits of Jobst Plankfelt (see Plate 29) and Hans Pfaffroth (see Plate 32) probably came from this sketchbook. Later, when Dürer temporarily left the Low Countries to attend the Emperor's Coronation at Aachen, he took with him another sketchbook, of oblong format, in which he drew in silverpoint.

Fifteen sheets, most of them with drawings on the *recto* and the *verso*, have been preserved, dispersed in various collections. These drawings, the majority of which show great strength, have been published under the title *Sketchbook of the Journey to the Netherlands* ([1]). They include drawings of buildings executed with the precision of an architect, portraits, landscapes, a dog, the lion he saw in Ghent, etc. It affords a complete visual narrative of his journey. Often a landscape or some building is drawn side by side with a portrait on the same page, almost all the separate drawings being made at different times and in different places. Not all the portraits in the *Sketchbook* were done from life. Some were records of the charcoal drawings that he had sold.

Despite the detailed recording in the Diary of his financial transactions, Dürer was to be disappointed at the final material outcome of his visit to the Netherlands. At the end of his visit, after adding up his income and expenditure, he complains : "For the more part of my work I have received nothing"; and further on, he remarks : "In all my doings, spendings, sales and other dealings, in all my connexions with high and low, I have suffered loss".

Apart from any material gain he may have made, Dürer must have profited artistically from his visit. Whilst, as we have seen, he had exercised a considerable influence on the artists of the Low Countries, he himself must have benefited from the many works he saw and admired. His spirit must surely have been enriched through participation in the amazingly busy life of the towns of Flanders and Brabant. There are, however, some special considerations. Firstly, Dürer's journey to the Netherlands was not intended as a study tour, and in this respect it was entirely different from the journeys he had made to Italy a long time before. In Venice he was the young painter anxious to absorb the new art of Italy. When he arrived in Antwerp, he was nearly fifty years of age; his style had long been established and there was nothing he could learn from the artists of the Low Countries, not even from the most eminent of them, such as Massys, Gossaert and van Orley, even if they also looked for inspiration south of the Alps. On the contrary it was Dürer's art, an art still Gothic in spirit yet replete with Italian Renaissance forms and motifs, that was to help these artists to an understanding of the "new Italian manner".

Of course, Dürer is full of praise for the works of his Netherlandish colleagues. It would appear, however, that it was their technique rather than the virtues of their composition or invention that he appreciated. As far as the great masters of the fifteenth century

([1]) *Sketchbook of the Journey to the Netherlands*, London, 1968.

CHAPTER V

III. *Portrait of Lorenz Sterck*.   Isabella Stewart Gardner Museum, Boston, Mass.

are concerned, Dürer appreciated the greatness of their works, but saw them as works of art achieved by methods he had long outgrown. However he might praise their works, it is clear that the paintings he saw by a Roger van der Weyden or a Hugo van der Goes excited him less than those "things" made of gold and silver brought from Mexico by the *conquistadores*.

Nevertheless, Dürer found the journey to the Netherlands a deep and refreshing experience, and as such it cannot but have affected his art. What effect it may have had was due less to his contact with the artists and their works, than to the general atmosphere of the Low Countries ([1]). It would be no exaggeration to say that the period he spent in the Low Countries gave him new inspiration, and at a moment when inspiration had threatened to forsake him and his paintings were beginning to betray signs of weariness and lack of imagination. The spectacle of life in the young and flourishing, cosmopolitan city of Antwerp, with its constant processions and pageants; Dürer's meeting with different people in Antwerp and on his visits to Zeeland, Brussels, Bruges and Ghent; the countless things of curiosity and interest that he saw; his discussions with the Humanists at a time of greatest religious drama; and last but not least, the enormous number of works he was able to carry out after nature; all these things contributed towards infusing his art with new life and endowing him with a fresh vision.

And we observe how on his return to Nuremberg Dürer was to lose that vein of stylisation that had threatened, before his journey, to intrude too greatly into his art. By drawing after the model, his genius as a portrait painter was brought to full maturity, and henceforth, in the last years of his life, we see him devoting himself almost exclusively to the practice of portrait painting and engraving. Whatever Albrecht Dürer may have said himself, his journey to the Netherlands was no less profitable to him than to the artists he met there.

J.-A. GORIS
Georges MARLIER

[1] Max J. FRIEDLÄNDER. - *Albrecht Dürer*, Leipzig, 1921.

CHAPTER V

THE DIARY

On Thursday after Kilian's, I, Albrecht Dürer, at my own charges and costs, took myself and my wife away to the Netherlands. And the same day, after passing through Erlangen, we put up for the night at Baiersdorf and spent there 3 pounds less 6 pfennigs. Nex day, Friday, we came to Forchheim and there I paid 22 pf. for the convoy. Thence I journeyed to Bamberg where I presented the Bishop with a painting of the Virgin, a Life of the Virgin, an Apocalypse, and a florin's worth of engravings. He invited me as his guest, gave me a Toll-pass and three letters of introduction and paid my bill at the Inn, where I had spent about a florin. I paid 6 florins in gold to the boatman who took me from Bamberg to Frankfurt. Master Lukas Benedict and Hans the painter sent me wine. 4 pf. for bread and 13 pf. as leaving gifts. Then I travelled from Bamberg to Eltman and I showed my pass and they let me go toll-free. Thence we passed by Zeil. I spent in the meantime 21 pf. Next I came to Hassfurt and presented my pass and they let me go toll-free. I paid 1 fl. into the Bishop of Bamberg's Chancery. Next I came to Theres to the monastery, and I showed my pass and they also let me go on. Then we journeyed to Unter-Euerheim where I stayed the night and spent 1 pf. From thence we travelled to Mainberg and I presented my pass and they let me go toll-free. We came next to Schweinfurt, where Doctor Rebart invited me, and he gave us wine in the boat. They let me also pass toll-free. A roast fowl 10 pf.; 18 pf. in the kitchen and for the child. Then we travelled to Volkach and I showed my pass and journeyed on, and we came to Schwarzach and there we stopped the night and I spent 22 pf.

And on Monday we were up early and after travelling by Dettebach we came to Kitzingen; and there I showed my pass and they let me go and I spent 37 pf. Then we travelled on

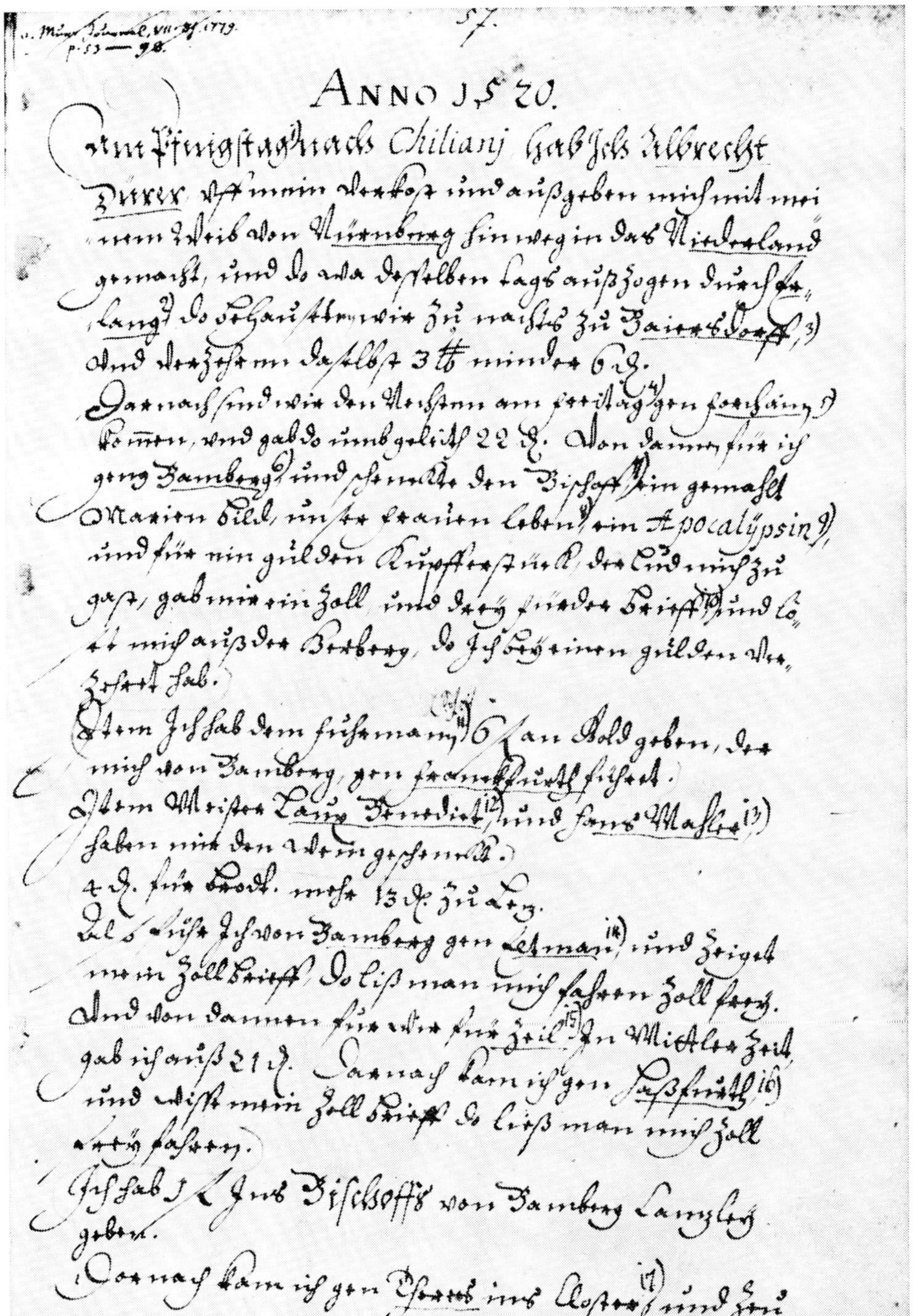

ANNO 1520.

Am Pfingstag nach Chiliani hab ich Albrecht
Dürer auf mein Unkost und Ausgeben mich mit mei-
nem Weib von Nürnberg hinweg in das Niederland
gemacht, und do an desselben tags ausgezogen durch...

[The remainder of the page consists of Dürer's Netherlands travel-diary entries in 16th-century German cursive, with marginal reference numbers (3, 4, 8, 9, 10, 11, 12, 13, 14, 15, 16, 17).]

The first page of Manuscript B. State Archives, Nuremberg (S. I., L 79, No. 15).

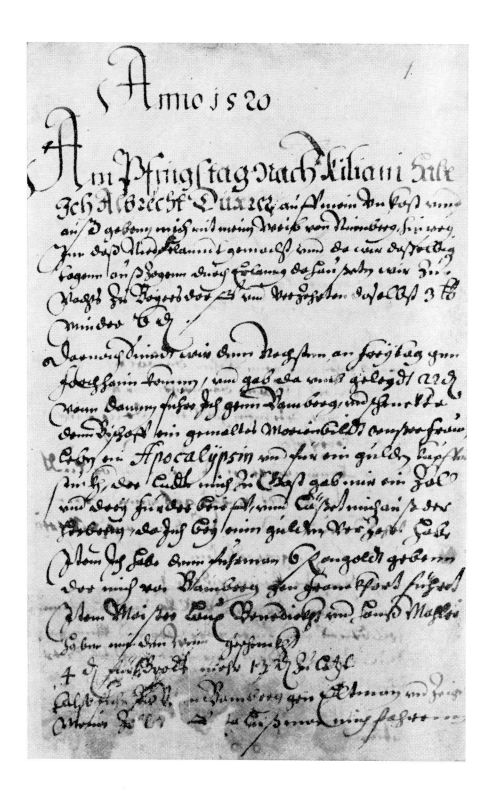

The first page of Manuscript A. State Library, Bamberg (J. H. Msc. art. 1).

past Sulzfeld to Marktbreit, and I showed my pass and they let me go; we went on past Frickenhausen to Ochsenfurt, there I showed my pass and there too they let me go. And we came to Eibelstadt, from that to Heidingsfeld, and from that to Würzburg. There I showed my pass and they let me go on. We went next to Erlabrunn and stopped the night there and I spent 22 pf. From that we journeyed on past Retzbach and Zellingen and came to Karlstadt; here I showed my pass and they let me go on. Then I travelled to Gmünden, and we breakfasted there and spent 22 pf. I also showed my pass and they let me go by. We travelled then to Hofstätten, I presented my pass and there they let me go. We came next to Lohr, where also I showed my pass and they let me go. Then we came to Neustadt and showed our pass and they let me go by. Also I paid 10 pf. for wine and crabs. And we came next to Rothenfels, and I showed my pass and they let me free. We stayed the night there and spent 20 pf.

Early on Wednesday we started off and passed by St Eucharius and came to Heidenfeld and then to Triefenstein. We next came to Homburg where I showed my pass and they let me go on; then we came to Wertheim and I showed my pass and they let me go off, and I spent 57 pf. We then went on to Prozelten, here I presented my pass and they let me go. Next we went on past Freudenberg, where I once more showed my pass and they let me go, and we came to Miltenberg and stayed the night there. And I showed my pass and they let me go and I spent 61 pf.

Next day we came to Klingenberg; I showed my pass and they let me go; and we came to Wörth, thence past Obernburg to Aschaffenburg. Here I presented my pass, and they let me go on, and I spent 52 pf. From that we journeyed to Seligenstadt, from there to Steinheim, where I showed my

St Eucharius. The monastery of Mattenstadt dedicated to the Saint.

pass and they let me go on. We stopped the night there with Johannes, who showed us the town and was very friendly towards us. I spent there 16 pf. So early on Friday we travelled to Kesselstadt, where I showed my pass and they let me go on. Then we came to Frankfurt and I showed my pass again and they let me go, and I spent 6 white-pfennigs and 1 1/2 Hellers. I gave the lad 2 white-pfennigs and I spent 6 white-pfennigs at night. Also Herr Jacob Heller gave me wine at the inn.

I have bargained to be taken from Frankfurt to Mainz with my goods for 1 fl. 2 white-pf. I also gave the lad 5 Frankfurt Hellers, and we spent 8 white-pf. for the night. On Sunday I travelled by the early boat from Frankfurt to Mainz, and on the way there we came to Höchst, where I presented my pass and they let me go on. I spent 8 Frankfurt pf. there. Thence we travelled to Mainz. I have also paid 1 white-pf. for landing my things, 14 Frankfurt Hellers to the boatman, and 18 pf. for a girdle. And I took passage in the Köln boat for myself and my things for 3 fl. I spent also at Mainz 17 white-pf. besides. Peter Goldschmidt, the Warden there, gave me two bottles of wine. Veit Varnbüler also invited me, but his Host would take no payment from him but insisted upon being my host himself, and they showed me much honour.

So I started away from Mainz, where the Main flows into the Rhine, and it was on the Monday after Magdalen's. I paid 10 Hellers for meat in the boat, and for eggs and pears 9 Hellers. Here too Leonard Goldschmidt gave me wine and birds in the boat to cook on the way to Köln. Master Jobst's brother likewise gave me a bottle of wine; and the Painters gave me two bottles of wine in the boat. We came then to Elfeld where I showed my pass and they took no toll; next we came to Rüdesheim. I paid also 2 white-pf. for bringing my things on board the boat. Then we came to Ehrenfels, and there I showed my pass but had to pay 2 fl. in gold. If however within two months I would bring them a free pass the toll-taker would give me back the 2 fl. in gold. After that we came to Bacharach, where I had to promise in writing that within two months I would either pay the toll or bring them a free-pass. We came next to Kaub and I showed my pass, but it would carry me no further, and I had to promise in writing as before. I spent there 11 Hellers. We then came to Sankt Goar, and here I showed my pass. The toll-taker asked me how they had treated me elsewhere. So I said I would pay him nothing. I paid 2 white-pf. to the messenger. We came after that to Boppart and I showed my pass at the Trier toll-bar, and was let go by; only I had to certify in a short writing under my seal that I had with me no common merchandise, and then the man willingly let me go. Next we came to Lahnstein and I showed my pass and the toll-taker let me go free, but he asked me to speak for him to my most gracious Lord of Mainz. He gave me also a can of wine, for he knew my wife well and was glad to see me. Then we came to Engers, which belongs to Trier, and I presented my pass and they let me go on toll-free. I said too that I would mention it to my Lord of Bamberg. We came next to Andernach, and I presented my pass and they let me go by free. I spent there 7 Hellers and 4 Hellers more.

On St James' day I travelled early from Andernach to Linz, and we went thence to the toll-station at Bonn, and there again they let me go by free. And so we came to Köln; and I spent in the boat 9 white-pf. and 1 more, and 4 pf. for fruit. At Köln I paid 7 white pf. for landing my things and I gave the boatmen 14 Hellers. And I gave my cousin Niklas my black fur-lined coat, edged with velvet, and to his wife I gave

Cousin Niklas. The goldsmith Niklas Dürer, called Unger, son of Dürer's uncle Ladislas.

a florin. At Köln Hieronymus Fugger gave me wine; Johann Grosserpecker also gave me wine; and my cousin Niklas, he also gave me wine. They gave us also a collation at the Barefoot convent, and one of the monks gave me a handkerchief. Herr Johann Grosserpecker has given me further 12 measures of the best wine. And I paid 2 white-pf. and 8 Hellers to the lad. I have spent besides at Köln 2 florins and 14 white-pf., and I have given away 10 white-pf., paid 3 pf. for fruit. Lastly I gave 1 white-pf. at leaving and paid 1 white-pf. to the messenger.

After that, on St Pantaleon's day, we travelled from Köln to a village called Büsdorf where we stayed over night and spent 3 white-pf. And we went on Sunday early to Rödingen; we had breakfast there and I spent 2 white-pf., and 3 pf., and again 3 pf. Then we came to Frei-Aldenhoven where we lay for the night, and there I spent 3 white-pf. We went on thence early in the morning to Freelenberg and passed the little town Gangelt, and breakfasted at a village called Süsterseel, and spent two white-pf. 2 Heller; further 1 white-pf. Again 2 white-pf. Thence we travelled to Sittard—a fine little town—and from there to Stockhem, which belongs to Liège. We had a pleasant inn here, and stayed the night and spent 4 white-pf.

And when we had crossed the Maas we started off early on Tuesday and came to Merten Lewbehen; there we had breakfast and spent 2 stivers, and I paid 1 white-pf. for a young fowl. We journeyed on thence across the heath and came to the Stosser, where we spent 2 st. and lay for the night. Early on Wednesday we went to West-Meerbeck. I bought 3 stivers' worth of bread and wine there and then we went to Branthoek, where we breakfasted and spent 1 st. Next we travelled to Uylenberg and we stopped there for the night and spent 3 st. 2 pf.   After that we went early on Thursday to Op ten Kruys and breakfasted there and spent 3 st. and we came next to Antwerp.

At Antwerp I went to Jobst Plankfelt's inn, and the same evening the Fuggers' Factor, Bernhard Stecher, invited me and gave us a costly meal.   My wife however dined at the inn. I paid the driver 3 gold florins for bringing us three, and 1 st. I paid for carrying the goods.   On Saturday after the feast of St Peter in Chains my host took me to see the Burgomaster's house at Antwerp.   It is newly built and beyond measure large, and very well ordered, with spacious and exceedingly beautiful chambers, a tower splendidly ornamented, a very large garden—altogether a noble house, the like of which I have nowhere seen in all Germany.   The house also is reached from both sides by a very long street, which has been quite newly built according to the Burgomaster's liking and at his charges.

I paid 3 st. to the messenger, 2 pf. for bread, 2 pf. for ink. On Sunday, it was St Oswald's day, the painters invited me to the hall of their guild, with my wife and maid.   All their service was of silver, and they had other splendid ornaments and very costly meats.   All their wives also were there.   And as I was being led to the table the company stood on both sides as if they were leading some great lord.   And there were amongst them men of very high position, who all behaved most respectfully towards me with deep courtesy, and promised to do everything in their power agreeable to me that they knew of.   And as I was sitting there in such honour the Syndic of Antwerp came, with two servants, and presented me with four cans of wine in the name of the Town Councillors of Antwerp, and they had bidden him say that they wished thereby to show their respect for me and to assure me of their

Jobst Plankfelt. Dürer made a number of portraits of his host. See Plate 29.

Bernhard Stecher. Head of the Augsburg Fugger's business in Antwerp.

The driver. Hans Staber, mentioned also on other occasions.

Us three. Dürer, his wife Agnes Frey and their maid-servant Susanna.

The Burgomaster's house. The Prinsenhof, in Prinsestraat, built for the Burgomaster Aert van Liere (died 1529), at present occupied by the Ecole Supérieure de Commerce Saint-Ignace.

Master Peeter. Peeter Teels, carpenter to the town and Cathedral (born 1467).

Master Quentin. The painter Quentin Massys (1466-1530).

Lorenz Staiber. Son of a Nuremberg merchant Hans Staiber, given noble rank by Henry VIII. Buried in the church of the monastery of Heilbronn. Dürer drew his coat-of-arms. See p. 81.

Portuguese Factor. João Brandão.

Portrait of my host. Now in the Städelsches Institut, Frankfurt. See Plate 29.

Triumphal way. Charles I of Spain, later Emperor Charles V, made his entry into Antwerp on the 23rd September 1520.

The Portuguese. The Portuguese Factor Brandão.

Alexander Imhof. Son of a Nuremberg nobleman, Veit Imhof. He lived from 1501 to 1546.

The small Passion. The twenty-seven plates of the "*Small*" *Passion*, the wood-cut series of 1511.

The Large Books. The *Apocalypse*, the series of twelve plates of the "*Large*" *Passion* and the *Life of the Virgin*.

Engraved Passions. The sixteen plates of the *Passion* engraved on copper.

good will. Wherefore I returned them my humble thanks and offered my humble service. After that came Master Peeter, the town-carpenter, and presented me with two cans of wine, with the offer of his willing services. So when we had spent a long and merry time together till late in the night, they accompanied us home, with lanterns in great honour. And they begged me to be ever assured and confident of their good will, and promised that in whatever I did they would be all-helpful to me. So I thanked them and laid me down to sleep.

I have also been in Master Quentin's house, and to the three great shooting places. I received a costly feast at Lorenz Staiber's, and another time at the Portuguese Factor's whose portrait I drew in charcoal. Of my host, Jobst Plankfelt, I have also made a portrait; he gave me a branch of white coral. Paid 2 st. for butter, 2 st. to the joiner at the Painters' warehouse. My host took me to the workshop in the Painters' warehouse at Antwerp, where they are making the Triumphal way through which King Charles is to make his entry. It is four hundred arches long, and each arch is 40 feet wide. They are to be set up along both sides of the street, handsomely ordered and two storeys high. The plays are to be acted on them. It will cost the Painters and Joiners altogether 4000 florins. "Auch wird man das als vol darzu brennen", and the whole work is very splendidly done.

I have dined again with the Portuguese and also once with Alexander Imhof. Sebald Fischer bought of me at Antwerp 16 small Passions for 4 fl., 32 of the Large Books for 8 fl., 6 engraved Passions for 3 fl., half-sheets—20 of all kinds taken together at 1 fl.—of these he took 3 fl. worth and again 5 1/4 fl. worth, quarter-sheets—45 of all kinds at 1 fl.—for 5 1/4 fl., and of whole-sheets 8 of all kinds taken together for 1 fl. It is paid. I have sold my host a Madonna painted on a small canvas for 2 fl. Rhenish. I took the portrait of Felix Hungersberg, the luteplayer, for the second time. Paid 1 st. for pears and bread, 2 st. to the barber. I also paid 14 st. for three small panels, besides 14 st. for laying the white ground and preparing the same. Further I have dined once with Alexander, the goldsmith, and once with Felix. Master Joachim has once dined with me, and his apprentice once. I made a drawing in half colours for the painters. I have taken 1 florin for expenses. I gave the four new little pieces to Peter Wolfgang. Master Joachim's apprentice has again dined with me. I gave Master Joachim 1 fl. worth of prints for lending me his apprentice and his colours, and I gave his apprentice three pounds' worth of prints. I have sent Alexander the goldsmith the four new pieces. I made portraits in charcoal of these Genoese :—Tomasin Florianus Romanus, native of Lucca, and Tomasin's two brothers Vincentius and Gerhard by name, all three Bombelli. I have dined with Tomasin thus often //////////. The Treasurer also gave me a child's head on linen, and a wooden weapon from Calicut, and one of the light wood reeds. Tomasin too has given me a plaited hat of alder bark. I dined once with the Portuguese, and have given a brother of Tomasin's 3 fl. worth of engravings. Herr Erasmus has given me a small Spanish "mantilla" and three men's portraits. Tomasin's brother gave me a pair of gloves. I have once more taken the portrait of Tomasin's brother Vincentius, and I gave Master Augustin Lombard the two parts of the "Imagines". I also took a portrait of the crooked-nosed Italian named Opitius. My wife and maid dined one day at Herr Tomasin's house; that makes 4 dinners. The Church of our Lady at Antwerp is so very large that many masses are sung in it at one time without interfering with

Felix Hungersberg. Captain of the Empire and a musician. Dürer drew his portrait on a number of occasions. See Plates 31 and 67.

Alexander, the goldsmith. Probably Alexander of Bruchsal, citizen of Antwerp from 1505. Another goldsmith by the name of Alexander was admitted to the Guild of Saint Luke in 1516.

Felix. Felix Hungersberg (see above).

Master Joachim. The painter Joachim Patinir, from Dinant. He was admitted to the Guild of Saint Luke in Antwerp in 1505, and died in 1516.

His apprentice. Dürer writes : "*sein Knecht*", "his lad", but the meaning is clear.

Four new little pieces. Four engravings, two of which, the Virgin crowned by an Angel and the Virgin and Child in swaddling clothes, are dated in 1520.

Master Joachim. The painter Joachim Patinir (see above).

Tomasin Florianus Romanus. Tomaso Bombelli, wealthy silk merchant.

Treasurer. Lorenz Sterck, Treasurer to the Provinces of Brabant and Antwerp from 1514 to 1525. See Plate III, p. 45.

Herr Erasmus. Erasmus of Rotterdam.

Augustin Lombard. Agostino Scarpinello, Secretary to Aloisio Marliano, Bishop of Tuy, sent as Milanese Ambassador to the English Court in 1524.

Imagines. *Imagines coeli septentrionalis et meridionalis*, woodcuts.

each other. The altars have wealthy endowments, and the best musicians are employed that can be had. The church has many devout services, much stone-work, and in particular a beautiful tower. I have also been into the rich Abbey of St Michael. There are, in the choir there, splendid stalls of sculptured stone-work. But at Antwerp they spare no cost on such things, for there is money enough.

I took the portrait of Herr Niclas, an Astronomer. He lives with the King of England, and has been very helpful and useful to me in many matters. He is a German, a native of Munich. I also made the portrait of Tomasin's daughter, Mistress Zoetje by name. Hans Pfaffroth gave me 1 Philips fl. for taking his portrait in charcoal. I have dined once more with Tomasin. My host's brother-in-law entertained me and my wife once. I changed 2 light florins for 24 st. for living expenses, and I gave 1 st. "trinkgeld" to a man who let me see an altar-piece. On the Sunday after Our Dear Lady's Assumption I saw the great Procession from the Church of Our Lady at Antwerp, when the whole town of every craft and rank was assembled, each dressed in his best according to his rank. And all ranks and guilds had their signs, by which they might be known. In the intervals great costly pole-candles were borne, and their long old Frankish trumpets of silver. There were also in the German fashion many pipers and drummers. All the instruments were loudly and noisily blown and beaten. I saw the Procession pass along the street, the people being arranged in rows, each man some distance from his neighbour, but the rows close one behind another. There were the Goldsmiths, the Painters, the Masons, the Broderers, the Sculptors, the Joiners, the Carpenters, the Sailors, the Fishermen, the Butchers, the Leatherers, the Clothmakers, the Bakers, the Tailors, the Cordwainers — indeed workmen of all kinds, and many craftsmen and dealers who work for their livelihood. Likewise the shopkeepers and merchants and their assistants of all kinds were there. After these came the shooters with guns, bows, and cross-bows and the horsemen and foot-soldiers also. Then followed the watch of the Lords Magistrates. Then came a fine troop all in red, nobly and splendidly clad. Before them however went all the religious Orders and the members of some foundations very devoutly, all in their different robes. A very large company of widows also took part in this procession. They support themselves with their own hands and observe a special rule. They were all dressed from head to foot in white linen garments, made expressly for the occasion, very sorrowful to see. Among them I saw some very stately persons. Last of all came the Chapter of Our Lady's Church with all their clergy, scholars, and treasurers. Twenty persons bore the image of the Virgin Mary with the Lord Jesus, adorned in the costliest manner, to the honour of the Lord God. In this Procession very many delightful things were shown, most splendidly got up. Waggons were drawn along with masques upon ships and other structures. Behind them came the company of the Prophets in their order and scenes from the New Testament, such as the Annunciation, the Three Holy Kings riding on great camels and on other rare beasts, very well arranged; also how Our Lady fled to Egypt—very devout—and many other things, which for shortness I omit. At the end came a great Dragon which St Margaret and her maidens led by a girdle; she was especially beautiful. Behind her came St George with his squire, a very goodly knight in armour. In this host also rode boys and maidens most finely and splendidly dressed in the costumes of many lands, representing various Saints. From beginning to end the Procession lasted more than two hours before it was gone past our house.   And so many things were there that I could never write them all in a book, so I let it well alone.

I have been into Fugger's house at Antwerp.   He has newly built it in very costly fashion, with a noteworthy tower, broad and high, and with a beautiful garden.   I saw also his fine horses.   Tomasin gave my wife 14 ells of good thick arras for a mantle and 3 1/2 ells of half-satin to line it.   I drew a design for a lady's forehead-band for the Goldsmith.   The Factor of Portugal sent me Portuguese and French wine to the inn. Signor Rodrigo of Portugal has given me a small cask full of all sorts of sweetmeats, amongst them a box of sugar-candy, besides two large dishes of barley-sugar, Marzipan, and many other kinds of sugarwork, some sugar-canes also as they grow.   I gave his servant in return 1 fl. for "trinkgeld".   I have again changed for my expenses 1 light florin for 12 st. The pillars in the parish Church in the Convent of St Michael at Antwerp are all made out of single blocks of beautiful black touch-stone.   Herr Ægidius, King Charles's Porter, has taken for me from Antwerp the "St Jerome in the Cell", the "Melancholy", the three new "Marys", the "Anthony", and the "Veronica" as a present for Master Konrad the good sculptor, whose like I have not seen.   He is in the service of Lady Margaret, the Emperor's daughter.   Also I gave Master Ægidius a "Eustace" and a "Nemesis".

I owe my host 7 fl. 20 st. 1 Heller—that was on Sunday before Bartholomew's.   For sitting-room and bedroom and bedding I am to pay him 11 fl. a month.   I came to a new agreement with my host on the 20th day of August—it was on Monday before Bartholomew's.   I am to eat with him and to pay 2 st. for the meal and extra for what is drunk.   My wife however and the maid can cook and eat up here.   I gave the Factor of Portugal a small carved Child, also an "Adam

Fuggers' house. It stood on the Steenhouwersvest.

The Factor of Portugal. Brandão.

Rodrigo of Portugal. Rodrigo Fernandez d'Almada, a wealthy Portuguese merchant and Portuguese Factor at Antwerp in 1521. His portrait, drawn with the brush, is in the Berlin Print Room. A charcoal portrait, in the same collection, is also considered to represent Rodrigo. See Plate 49.

Herr Ægidius. Gilles von Apfennauwe, called "the German", a Gentleman at the Imperial Court.

Master Konrad. The sculptor Konrad Meit, who executed among other things the Tomb of Marguerite of Austria at Brou.

Eustace. Dürer's engraving of Saint Eustace (c. 1500).

Nemesis. The engraving called the "Large" Fortuna.

Small carved Child. The phrase employed by Dürer, "ein kleines geschniedenes Kindlein", could refer to an engraving or carving.

and Eve", the "Jerome in the Cell", the "Hercules", the "Eustace", the "Melancholy", the "Nemesis"; then of the half-sheets—three new "Marys", the "Veronica", the "Anthony", the "Nativity", and the "Cross"; also the best of the quarter-sheets, eight in number; then the three Books—"Our Lady's Life", the "Apocalypse", and the "Great Passion"; and lastly the "Little Passion", and the "Passion" engraved on copper—altogether that is 5 fl. worth. I gave the same quantity to Signor Rodrigo, the other Portuguese. Rodrigo has given my wife a small green parrot.

On Sunday after Bartholomew's I travelled with Herr Tomasin from Antwerp to Mechlin, where we lay for the night. There I bade Master Konrad and a painter with him to supper. And this Master Konrad is the good carver in Lady Margaret's service. From Mechlin we passed through the little town Vilvorde and came to Brussels on Monday at midday. I have paid the messenger 3 st. I dined with my Lords at Brussels, also once with Herr Bonysius and I gave him a "Passion" in copper. I gave the Margrave Hans at Brussels the letter of recommendation which my Lord of Bamberg wrote for me, and I gave him a "Passion" engraved in copper, by which to remember me. I have also dined again with my Lords of Nürnberg.

In the golden chamber in the Townhall at Brussels I saw the four paintings which the great Master Roger made. And I saw out behind the King's house at Brussels the fountains, labyrinth, and Beast-garden; anything more beautiful and pleasing to me and more like a Paradise I have never seen. Erasmus is the name of the little man who wrote out my supplication at Herr Jacob Bonysius' house. At Brussels is a very splendid Townhall, large, and covered with beautiful carved stonework, and it has a noble, open tower. I took a

Master Konrad. The sculptor Konrad Meit (see above).

My Lords. The Ambassadors of Nuremberg charged with carrying the Insignia of the Empire at the Coronation at Aachen.

Herr Bonysius. Jacopo dei Banissi, Secretary to the Emperor Maximilian and a friend of Pirckheimer. He died in 1532.

Margrave Hans. Johann, Margrave of Brandenburg, who had married the widow of Ferdinand of Aragon.

Master Roger. The painter Roger van der Weyden (c. 1400-1464). The paintings represented the Justice of Emperor Trajan, Pope Gregory the Great discovering the remains of Emperor Trajan, the Justice of King Erkenbald and the death of the King.

A Paradise. Dürer's drawing of the park is in the Academy in Vienna. See Plate 75.

Erasmus. Erasmus Sternberger, secretary to Jacopo dei Banissi.

portrait at night by candlelight of Master Konrad of Brussels, who was my host; I drew at the same time Doctor Lamparter's son in charcoal, also the hostess. I saw the things which have been brought to the King from the new land of gold, a sun all of gold a whole fathom broad, and a moon all of silver of the same size, also two rooms full of the armour of the people there, and all manner of wondrous weapons of theirs, harness and darts, very strange clothing, beds, and all kinds of wonderful objects of human use, much better worth seeing than prodigies. These things were all so precious that they are valued at 100,000 florins. All the days of my life I have seen nothing that rejoiced my heart so much as these things, for I saw amongst them wonderful works of art, and I marvelled at the subtle Ingenia of men in foreign lands. Indeed I cannot express all that I thought there. At Brussels I saw many other beautiful things besides, and especially I saw a fish bone there, as vast as if it had been built up of squared stones. It was a fathom long and very thick, it weighs up to 15 cwt., and its form resembles that drawn here. It stood up behind on the fish's head. I was also in the Count of Nassau's house which is very splendidly built and as beautifully adorned. I have again dined // with my Lords.

Lady Margaret sent after me to Brussels and promised to speak for me to King Charles, and she has shown herself quite exceptionally kind to me. I sent her my engraved "Passion" and another copy to her treasurer, Jan Marnix by name, and I took his portrait in charcoal. I gave 2 st. for a buffalo ring, also 2 st. for opening St Luke's picture. When I was in the Nassau house in the chapel there, I saw the good picture that Master Hugo painted, and I saw the two fine large halls and the treasures everywhere in the house, also the great bed wherein 50 men can lie. And I saw the great stone which the storm

New land of gold. Mexico.

Jan Marnix. Jean de Marnix, "Seigneur" of Marnix and Toulouse, counsellor and treasurer to the Regent Marguerite.

Master Hugo. The painter Hugo van der Goes (c. 1440-1482).

cast down in the field near the Lord of Nassau. The house stands high, and from it there is a most beautiful view, at which one cannot but wonder; and I do not believe that in all the German lands the like of it exists.

Master Bernard, the painter, invited me and prepared so costly a meal that I do not think 10 fl. will pay for it. Lady Margaret's Treasurer, whom I drew, and the King's Steward, Jean de Metenye by name, and the Town-Treasurer named Van Busleyden invited themselves to it, to get me good company. I gave him a "Passion" engraved in copper, and he gave me in return a black Spanish bag worth 3 fl. I have also given Erasmus of Rotterdam a "Passion" engraved in copper. I gave a "Passion" engraved in copper to Erasmus, Panisius' secretary. The man at Antwerp who gave me the "Child's" head is named Lorenz Sterck. I took the portrait in charcoal of Master Bernard, Lady Margaret's painter. I have once more taken Erasmus of Rotterdam's portrait. I gave Lorenz Sterck a sitting "Jerome" and the "Melancholy", and took a portrait of my hostess's godmother. Six people whose portraits I drew at Brussels have given me nothing. I paid 3 st. for two buffalo horns and 1 st. for two Eulenspiegels.

So then on Sunday after St Giles' day I travelled with Herr Tomasin to Mechlin and took leave of Herr Hans Ebner, and he would take nothing for my expenses while I was with him— 7 days. I paid 1 st. for Hans Geuder. 1 st. I gave to my host's servant for a leaving gift. At Mechlin I supped with the Lady of Nieuwekerke, and early on Monday I started away from the town and travelled to Antwerp.

I dined early with the Portuguese. He gave me three pieces of porcelain and Rodrigo gave me some Calicut feathers. I have spent 1 fl. and paid the messenger 2 st. I bought Susanna a mantle for 2 fl. 10 st. My wife paid 4 fl. Rhenish for a wash-

Master Bernard. The painter Bernard van Orley (1493-1542).

Jean de Metenye. Burgomaster of Bruges and Grand Marshal of the Emperor.

Van Busleyden. Gilles of Busleyden, Treasurer of the Church of Sainte-Gudule in Brussels.

Panisius. Banissi, also called Bonysius (see above).

Lorenz Sterck. Treasurer to Brabant and Antwerp (see above).

Erasmus of Rotterdam. The drawing in charcoal is in the Louvre. See Plate 55.

Eulenspiegels. Refers either to the popular book or to an engraving by Lukas van Leyden.

Herr Tomasin. Bombelli.

Hans Ebner. One of the town-councillors of Nuremberg, who attended the Coronation of Emperor Charles V.

Hans Geuder. Eldest son of Martin Geuder and his wife, a sister of Pirckheimer. He became a Nuremberg councillor.

The Portuguese. The Portuguese Factor Brandão.

Rodrigo. Rodrigo Fernandez d'Almada (see above).

Susanna. Dürer's maid-servant, who later married his pupil Georg Pencz.

The two Lords of Rogendorf. Wilhelm and Wolfgang of Rogendorf. The first (1481-1541) was Lieutenant of Friesland and became, after the death of Emperor Maximilian, one of the Regents of the Low Countries; the second (1483-1543) was a Marshal in Austria in 1527.

Their arms. A damaged copy of the engraving is preserved in the Germanisches Nationalmuseum, Nuremberg.

Jakob Rehlinger. Member of an important Augsburg Family.

Duke Friedrich. Frederick II (1482-1556). He was at the Brussels Court from 1501; Prince-Elector in 1544.

Panisio. Jacopo dei Banissi (see above).

The new Peasants. A copper-engraving of 1519 representing peasants at a market.

Master Marc. Marc de Glasere of Bruges, goldsmith to the Regent Marguerite from 1524-1525.

Hönigin. It has not been possible to identify this glasspainter.

Master Dierick. Dirck Jacobsz Vellert (Felert), member of the Guild of Saint Luke at Antwerp in 1511 and Dean in 1518 and 1526.

tub, a bellows, a bowl, her slippers, fire-wood, knee-hose, a parrot-cage, two jugs, and "trinkgelds". She has spent besides for eating, drinking, and other necessaries 21 st.

Now on Monday after Giles' I have again come into Jobst Plankfelt's house, and I have dined with him as many times as I have here marked ////////////////. I gave Niklas, Tomasin's man, 1 st. I paid 5 st. for the little frame, and 1 st. more. My host gave me an Indian cocoanut and an old Turkish whip. Thus often have I dined with Tomasin ////////////. The two Lords of Rogendorf invited me. I dined once with them and drew their arms large on a wood-block for cutting.

I have given away 1 st. My wife has changed 1 fl. for 24 st. for expenses. I gave 2 st. for a "trinkgeld". I dined once in the Fuggers' house with young Jakob Rehlinger, and I have also once more dined with him. My wife has again changed 1 fl. for 24 st. for expenses. I gave an engraved "Jerome" and the two new half-sheets—the "Mary" and the "Anthony"—to Wilhelm Hauenhut, servant of my lord Duke Friedrich the Palgrave. I gave Herr Jacob Panisio a good painting of a Veronica face, a "Eustace", the "Melancholy", and a "Sitting Jerome", the "St Anthony", the two new "Marys" and the new "Peasants". Then I sent to his secretary, Erasmus, who drew out the Request for me, a "Sitting Jerome", the "Melancholy", the "Anthony", and the two new "Marys". And what I have given them is worth 7 fl. in all. I gave Master Marc, the Goldsmith, a "Passion" in copper and he gave me 3 fl. in payment. I have besides received 3 fl. 20 st. for prints. To the glasier Hönigin I gave 4 little engravings. I have dined with Herr Panisio ///. I paid 4 st. for carbon and black-chalk. 1 fl. 8 st. I paid for wood and spent 3 st. more. This number of times have I dined with my Lords of Nürnberg, //////////. Master Dierick, the glasspainter, sent me the red colour that is found at Antwerp in the new bricks. I made a portrait in charcoal of Master Jacob of Lübeck, he gave my wife a Philips fl. I have again changed a Philips fl. for expenses. I presented a "Sitting Jerome" engraved in copper to Lady Margaret. I sold a woodcut "Passion" for 12 st., and an "Adam and Eve" for 4 st. Captain and Luteplayer Felix has bought of me for 8 fl. in gold a large engraving, a woodcut "Passion" and an engraved "Passion", 2 half-sheets, and 2 quarter-sheets. So I gave him another large engraving. I took a charcoal portrait of Herr Panisius. Rodrigo gave me another parrot and I gave his lad 2 st. for "trinkgeld". I gave Johann Van den Winkel, the trumpeter, a small woodcut "Passion", a "Jerome in the Cell", and a "Melancholy". I paid 6 st. for a pair of shoes. I paid 5 st. for a sea-rod fish, and Georg Schlaudersbach gave me another which cost 6 st. I dined once with Wolf Haller, who used to be the Fuggers' servant, when he had invited my Lords of Nürnberg. For art-wares I have received 2 Philips fl. 6 st. I have again dined once with my wife. 1 st. I gave to Hans Dener's lad for a "trinkgeld". I have taken 100 st. for art-wares. Then I made a charcoal portrait of Master Jacob, von Rogendorf's painter; and I have drawn for von Rogendorf his arms upon wood, for which he gave me 7 ells of velvet. I dined once again with the Portuguese. I took the portrait of Master Jan Prost of Bruges and he gave me 1 fl.—it was done in charcoal. 23 st. I paid for a back of fur. I sent Hans Schwarz 2 fl. in gold for my picture, in a letter by the Antwerp Fuggers to Augsburg. I bought a red woollen shirt for 31 st. I gave 2 st. for the colour which is found in the bricks, and I paid 9 st. for an ox-horn. I took the portrait of a Spaniard in charcoal. Dined once with my wife. I bought a dozen little pipes for 1 st. I paid 3 st. for two little veined shells; Felix has given my

Master Jacob of Lübeck. Painter to the Rogendorfs.

Felix. Felix Hungersberg (see above).

Panisius. Jacopo dei Banissi (see above). A drawing in black chalk in the Rijksmuseum in Amsterdam has been identified as a portrait of Banissi. See Plate 57.

Georg Schlaudersbach. A nobleman of Nuremberg (1496-1552).

Wolf Haller. A representative of the Fuggers, living in Antwerp. He became Treasurer to the Regent Mary of Hungary (1492-1559).

Master Jan Prost of Bruges. The painter Jan Prevost of Bruges (died 1529), whose Last Judgment is in Bruges Museum.

My picture. The medallion portrait of Dürer made by Hans Schwarz still exists.

Little pipes. The meaning is not clear (pipes or flutes?).

Printed "Entry into Antwerp". Peter Ægidius' " Triumph", a description of the Triumphal Entry of Emperor Charles V.

Bones of the giant. The bones of the legendary giant Druon Antigoon. The bones, preserved in the Steen Museum in Antwerp, are actually those of a whale.

Raphael. The great Italian master died on the 6th April 1520.

Tommaso of Bologna. Tommaso Vincidor of Bologna. Sent to the Netherlands by Pope Leo X. He built the Nassau Palace in Breda. He died before 1536.

Niklas Ziegler. Of Nördlingen, Vice-Chancellor to Emperor Charles V (died 1534).

wife two like them; and Master Jacob, the painter from Lübeck, has also given my wife another. Dined once with Rogendorf. I have paid 1 st. for the printed "Entry into Antwerp" telling how the King was received with a splendid triumph—the gates very costly adorned—and with plays, great joy, and graceful maidens whose like I have seldom seen. I changed 1 fl. for expenses. I saw at Antwerp the bones of the giant. His leg above the knee is 5 1/2 ft. long and beyond measure heavy and very thick, so with his shoulder blades—a single one is broader than a strong man's back—and his other limbs. The man was 18 ft. high, had ruled at Antwerp and done wondrous great feats, as is more fully written about him in an old book, which the Lords of the Town possess.

The studio of Raphael of Urbino has quite broken up since his death, but one of his scholars, Tommaso of Bologna by name, a good painter, desired to see me. So he came to me and has given me an antique gold ring with a very well cut stone. It is worth 5 fl. but already I have been offered the double for it. I gave him 6 fl. worth of my best prints for it. I bought a piece of calico for 3 st.; I paid the messenger 1 st.; 3 st. I spent in company. I have presented a whole set of all my works to Lady Margaret the Emperor's daughter, and have drawn her two pictures on parchment with the greatest pains and care. All this I set at as much as 30 fl. And I have had to draw the design of a house for her physician the Doctor, according to which he intends to build one; and for drawing that I would not care to take less than 10 fl. I have given the servant 1 st., and paid 1 st. for brick-colour. I gave Herr Niklas Ziegler a Body of Christ lying dead; it is worth 3 fl. To the Portuguese Factor I gave a painting of the Child's head worth 1 fl. I bought a small buffalo horn for 10 st. I paid 1 gold fl. for an elk's hoof.

I made a portrait in charcoal of Master Adrian. I gave 2 st. for the "Condemnation" and the "Dialogus" and 3 st. to the messenger. To Master Adrian I gave 2 fl. worth of art-wares. Bought a piece of red chalk for 1 st. I have taken Herr Wolf von Rogendorf's portrait with the metal-point. I gave away 3 st. I made the portrait of a noble lady at Tomasin's house. To Niclas I gave a "Jerome in the Cell" and the two new "Marys". On Monday after Michaelmas 1520, I gave Thomas of Bologna a whole set of prints to send for me to Rome to another painter who should send me Raphael's work in return. I dined once with my wife. I paid 3 st. for the little tracts. The Bolognese has made my portrait, he means to take it with him to Rome. I bought an elk's foot for 3 st., and I have paid 2 gold fl. 4 st. for Herr Hans Ebner's panel. Dined out. I exchanged a crown for expenses. Dined out. I am taking 11 fl. with me for my expenses to Aachen. From Ebner I have received 2 fl. 4 st. Paid 9 st. for wood. Gave Meyding 20 st. to send my box. I took the portrait of a lady of Bruges; she gave me a Philips fl. I gave away 3 st. on leaving, paid 2 st. for varnish, 1 st. for stone colour. I paid 13 st. to the furrier, 1 st. for leather. I bought 2 mussels for 2 st. In Johann Gabriel's house I took the portrait of an Italian lord, and he gave me 2 gold fl. I bought a wallet for 2 fl. 4 st.

On Thursday after Michaelmas I started from Antwerp for Aachen, and took with me another florin and a rosenoble. After passing thro' Maastricht we came to Gulpen and thence on Sunday to Aachen. There, up till now, I have spent, with fare and all, 3 fl. At Aachen I saw the well-proportioned pillars with their good capitals of green and red porphyry and "Gossenstein" which Charles the Great had brought from Rome thither and there set up. They are correctly made according to Vitruvius' writings. I bought an ox-horn at

Master Adrian. Adriaen Herbouts, Syndic of the Town of Antwerp.

The Condemnation and the Dialogus. *Condemnatio doctrinae librorum M. Lutheri* etc. *cum responsione Lutheri. Ayn schöner Dialogus von Zwayen guten Gesellen, sagendt von Antechrist und seynen Jüngern* (1520).

Niclas. One of Bombelli's servants.

The Bolognese. Tommaso Vincidor of Bologna (see above). There is an engraving after the portrait (by A. Stock, 1629).

Hans Ebner's panel. It was on this panel that Dürer painted the portrait of Hans Ebner.

Meyding. Utz Hanolt Meyding, who was charged with sending Dürer's luggage to Nuremberg after the artist's departure from the Netherlands.

Well-proportioned pillars. The porphyry columns sent by Charlemagne to Aachen from Ravenna, and not from Rome.

Gossenstein. "Cast stone". Apparently an artificial stone of cement and chippings.

Vitruvius. Vitruvius' *De Architectura*.

Schlaudersbach. See above.

The Hall. The Coronation Hall at the Town Hall in Aachen.

Christoph Groland. (1508-1561.) Nuremberg Senator in 1549.

Peter von Enden. Burgomaster of Aachen in 1521.

Paulus Topler. Citizen of Nuremberg (1455-1544). See Plate 1.

Martin Pfinzing. Nuremberg Councillor (1490-1552). Commander in the war against the Turks in 1532 and 1542. The drawing is in the Berlin Print Room. See Plate 1.

The arm of the Emperor Heinrich. Dürer is apparently mistaken; he would have seen the arm of Charlemagne.

The shift and girdle of Our Lady. This relic is still preserved.

Sketch of the Church of Our Lady. This drawing of the cathedral is in the British Museum. See Plate 2.

Sturm. Caspar Sturm, the Imperial Herald who conducted Luther to the Diet of Worms. See Plate 4.

Sister of the Köpffingrin. Sister-in-law of Jacob Köpfinger of Ulm, a Nuremberg advocate.

Mathes. Matthias Püchler, an officer of the Imperial Chancellery who passed an application made by Dürer.

Stephan. Stefan Lullier, Librarian to Marguerite of Austria.

Aachen for 1 gold fl. I took the portraits of Hans Ebner and Georg Schlaudersbach in charcoal, and Hans Ebner's a second time. I paid 2 st. for a soft whetstone, and spent 5 st. on drinking with my travelling companions and for a bath. I have changed 1 fl. for expenses. I gave the town-servant who took me up into the Hall 2 white pf. I have spent 5 white pf. on a bath and for drinking in company. I lost 7 st. at play with Herr Hans Ebner. I have taken young Christoph Groland's portrait in charcoal, also that of my host Peter von Enden. I spent 3 st. in company and gave 1 st. to the messenger. I have drawn the portraits of Paulus Topler and Martin Pfinzing in my sketch-book. I have seen the arm of the Emperor Heinrich, the shift and girdle of Our Lady, and other relics. I sketched the Church of Our Lady with its surroundings. I took Sturm's portrait. I made the portrait in charcoal of Peter von Enden's brother-in-law. I bought a large ox-horn for 10 white pf. I gave 2 white pf. as "trinkgeld". I have changed another florin for expenses. I have lost 3 white pf. at play. Further lost 2 st. at play. Gave the messenger || white pf. I have given Tomasin's daughter the painted "Trinity"; it is worth 4 fl. I paid 1 st. for washing. I took the portrait of the sister of the Köpffingrin at Aachen, and again with the metal point. I spent 3 white pf. on a bath. I have paid 8 white pf. for a buffalo-horn; item, gave 2 white pf. for a girdle. I have paid 1 Philips fl. for a scarlet shawl, 6 pf. for paper. I have changed a florin for expenses. I paid 2 white pf. for washing.

On the 23rd day of October, King Charles was crowned at Aachen. There I saw all manner of lordly splendour, more magnificent than anything that those who live in our parts have seen—all, as it has been described. I gave Mathes 2 fl. worth of art-wares, and I gave Stephan, one of Lady Margaret's chamberlains,

3 prints. I bought a cedarwood rosary for 1 fl. 10 white pf. I gave 1 st. to little Hans in the stable, and 1 st. to the child in the house. I lost 2 1/2 st. at play; spent 2 st.; paid the barber 2 st. I have again changed 1 fl. I gave away 7 white pf. in the house at leaving and travelled from Aachen to Jüliers and thence to —. I paid 4 st. for two eyeglasses; played away 2 st. in an embossed silver king. I bought 2 ox-horns for 8 white pf.

On Friday before Simon and Jude's I left Aachen and travelled to Düren, and I went into the chuch there, in which St Anne's head is. Thence we went on and came on Sunday, Simon and Jude's day, to Köln. I had lodging, food, and drink at Brussels with my Lords of Nürnberg and they would take nothing from me for it; and at Aachen likewise I ate with them for three weeks and they have brought me to Köln and would take nothing from me.

I bought a tract of Luther's for 5 white pf. and the "Condemnation of Luther", the pious man, for 1 white pf.; also a rosary for 1 white pf. and a girdle for 2 white pf., a pound of candles for 1 white pf. I changed 1 fl. for expenses. I had to give my great ox-horn to Herr Leonhard Groland, and to Herr Hans Ebner I had to give my large rosary of cedarwood. Bought a pair of shoes for 6 white pf. I paid 2 white pf. for a little skull. 1 white pf. I gave for beer and a bread and 1 white pf. for braid. I have given 4 white pf. to two messengers. To Niklas' daughter I gave 2 white pf. for braid. Paid a messenger 1 white pf. I gave prints worth 2 fl. to Herr Ziegler's Linhard. I have paid the barber 2 white pf. I paid 2 white pf. for opening the picture at Köln which Master Stefan made. I gave the messenger 1 white pf. and spent 2 white pf. in drinking with my companions. I took a portrait of Gottschalk's sister. I bought a little tract for 1 white pf.

On Sunday evening after All Saints' Day in the year 1520, I saw

And thence to —. The name of the place is missing in the text.

Silver king. The next is not clear.

Condemnation. The *Condemnatio...* that Dürer had already bought in Antwerp (see above).

Braid. The text is not clear and the word "*Euspertele*" has probably been misread.

Linhard. A secretary to Ziegler, Imperial Vice-Chancellor.

The picture at Köln. Stefan Lochner's famous altarpiece, at the time in the chapel of the Town Hall and now in the Cathedral.

Staiber. Lorenz Staiber (see above).

Duke Friedrich. Count Palatine (see above).

Niklas Haller. Burgomaster of Nuremberg, was one of the delegation sent by the town of Nuremberg to the Coronation (1481-1528).

St Ursula's church. Where the relics of 11,000 Virgins are kept.

Förherwerger. Possibly Stemberger, secretary to Banissi.

Confirmation. Dürer received an Imperial pension of 100 florins per year. The confirmation of his pension granted him this sum for the remainder of his life, the moneys to be paid out of the contributions made by the town of Nuremberg to the Emperor.

a nobles' dance and banquet in Emperor Charles's dancing-house. It was spendidly done. I drew for Staiber his arms on a wood-block. I gave a "Melancholy" to a young Count at Köln, and the new "Mary" to Duke Friedrich. I took Niklas Haller's portrait in charcoal and gave 2 white pf. to the door-porter. I bought two little tracts for 3 white pf. and gave 10 white pf. for a cow-horn. At Köln I went to St Ursula's church and to her grave, and saw the great relics of the holy maid and the others. Förherwerger's portrait I took in charcoal. I changed 1 fl. for expenses. I gave Niklas' wife 8 white pf. when she invited me as guest. I bought two prints for 1 st. Herr Hans Ebner and Herr Niklas Groland would take no payment from me for 8 days at Brussels, 3 weeks at Aachen, and 14 days at Köln. I have made the nun's portrait. I gave the nun 7 white pf. and 3 half-sheet engravings.

My confirmation from the Emperor came to my Lords of Nürnberg for me on Monday after Martin's in the year 1520 after great trouble and labour. I gave Niklas' daughter 7 white pf. at leaving and 1 fl. to his wife and again 1/4 fl. to his daughter at leaving, and I started away from Köln. Before that Staiber invited me once as guest, and my cousin Niklas once, and old Wolfgang once, and once besides I dined as guest. I gave Niklas' man a "Eustace" at leaving, and to his little daughter another 1/4 fl., for they had much trouble with me. I bought a little ivory skull for 1 fl. and a small turned box for 1 white pf., also a pair of shoes for 7 white pf. and lastly I gave Niklas' man a "Nemesis".

I started off early by boat from Köln on Wednesday after Martin's and went as far as —. I paid 6 white pf. for a pair of shoes. I have given 4 white pf. to the messenger. From Köln I went by the Rhine to Zons, from Zons to Neuss, and from thence to Zum Stein, where we stayed the day and I spent

Old copy of Charles V's confirmation of the Imperial pension of 100 Rhenish florins granted by Emperor Maximilian to Dürer. Town Archives, Nuremberg.

Old copy of Charles V's confirmation of the Imperial pension of 100 Rhenish florins granted by Emperor Maximilian to Dürer. Town Archives, Nuremberg.

6 white pf.   Then we went to a little town, Düsseldorf; I spent 2 white pf.   Thence we went to Kaiserswerth, thence to Duisberg another little town; and we passed two castles one called Angerort and the other Ruhrort.   Thence we went to Orsoy, a little town, thence to Rheinberg, another little town, and there I stayed the night and spent 6 white pf.   From thence I went to these little towns : first Burg Wesel, then Rees, after that to Emmerich; we came next to Thomas and from there to Nymwegen, I travelled to Tiel, from there to Herzogenbosch. At Emmerich I stopped and had an excellent meal for 3 white pf. And there I took the portrait of a goldsmith's apprentice, Peter Federmacher of Antwerp, and a woman.   The reason of our stay at Emmerich was that a very great storm of wind fell on us.   I spent besides 5 white pf. and changed 1 fl. for expenses; also I took the host's portrait, and we only reached Nymwegen on Sunday.   I paid the boatman 20 white pf.   Nymwegen is a fine town, it has a beautiful church and a well-placed castle.   From thence we went to Tiel; there we left the Rhine and sailed up the Maas to Heerewaarden, where the two towers stand.   We spent the night there and this day I spent 7 st.   On Tuesday we went on early up the Maas to Bommel; a great storm of wind came on there, so we hired cart-horses and rode without saddles to Herzogenbosch.   I paid 1 fl. for the journey in the boat and on horse.   Bosch is a fine town and has a most beautiful chuch.   It is very strongly fortified.   I spent 10 st. there, although Master Arnold paid for the meal for me.   The goldsmiths came to see me and they did me much honour.
After that we went off early on Ladyday and passed thro' the very large and beautiful village of Oosterwyck; we breakfasted however at Tilborg and I spent 4 white pf.   We came next to Baarle, stopped the night, and I spent 5 st. there, but my companions quarelled with the host so we went on in the night to

Thomas. It should read : "*Tholhüs*", the toll-house at Lobit. See Plate 4.

Master Arnold. Arnold von Seligenstadt. His portrait, drawn with the pen, is in the Musée Bonnat in Bayonne. See Plate 37.

Assumption. The text reads, erroneously : "after [the] Assumption", but should read : "after the Presentation of the Virgin" (the 21st November).

Niklas Sopalis. It has not been possible to identify this person.

Assumption. See above.

Hoogstraten. We stopped there 2 hrs. and then went by St Leonhardskirchen to Harscht; we breakfasted there and I spent 4 st. We went on thence to Antwerp and I paid the driver 15 st.; that was on Thurday after Our Lady's Assumption. I gave an engraved "Passion" to Johann, Jobst's brother-in-law's servant, and I made Niklas Sopalis' portrait. On the Thursday after the day of Our Lady's Assumption 1520, I came again into Jobst Plankfelt's house and have dined with him thus often ||||, my wife thus often ||. I have changed 1 fl. for expenses, further 1 crown. The seven weeks that I have been away my wife and maid have spent 7 crowns and bought other things besides to the value of 4 fl. I spent 4 st. in company. Six times have I dined with Tomasin. On St Martin's day in Our Lady's church at Antwerp some one cut off my wife's purse in which were 2 fl. The purse, besides what was in it, was worth another florin, and some keys were in it too.

On St Catharine's eve I paid my host 10 gold crowns for my reckoning. Thus often have I dined with the Portuguese ||. Rodrigo gave me 6 Indian nuts, so I gave his boy 2 st. for "trinkgeld". I paid 19 st. for parchment. 2 crowns have I changed for expenses. I have received 8 fl. in all for 2 prints of

"Adam and Eve", 1 "Sea-monster", 1 "Jerome", 1 "Knight", 1 "Nemesis", 1 "Eustace", 1 whole sheet, further 17 etched pieces, 8 quarter-sheets, 19 woodcuts, 7 of the bad woodcuts, 2 books, and 10 small woodcut "Passions". I gave the 3 Large Books for an ounce of "Schamloth". I have changed a Philips fl. for expenses, also my wife changed 1 fl. for expenses. At Zierikzee in Zeeland a whale has been stranded by a high tide and a gale of wind. It is much more than 100 fathoms long and no man living in Zeeland has seen one even a third as long as this is. The fish cannot get off the land; the people would gladly see it gone, as they fear the great stink, for it is so large that they say it could not be cut in pieces and the blubber boiled down in half a year. Stephan Capelle has given me a cedarwood rosary, for which I promised to take, and have taken his portrait. I bought some furnace-brown and a pair of snuffers for 4 st. I paid 3 st. for paper. I made a pen-and-ink portrait in his book of Felix kneeling. He gave me 100 oysters. I gave Herr Lazarus, the great man, an engraved "Jerome" and the three Large Books. Rodrigo gave me strong wine and oysters. I bought some black chalk for 7 white pf. I have had as guests at dinner Tomasin, Gerhard, Tomasin's daughter, her husband, the glass-painter Hennik, Jobst and his wife, and Felix. It cost 2 fl. Tomasin gave me 4 ells of grey damask for a doublet. I have again changed 1 Philips fl. for expenses.

On St Barbara's eve I rode away from Antwerp to Bergen, I paid 12 st. for the horse and spent 1 fl. 6 st. there. At Bergen I bought my wife a thin Netherlandish cloth for the head; it cost 1 fl. 7 st. Further 6 st. for three pair of shoes, 1 st. for a pair of spectacles, also 6 st. for an ivory button. I gave 2 st. for a "trinkgeld". I took the portraits in charcoal of Jan de Has, his wife, and his two daughters, and I drew the maid and the old woman with the metal-point in my sketch-book. I saw the von Bergen house, it is very large and beautifully built. Bergen is a pleasant place in summer and two great fairs are held there in the year.

On Our Lady's eve I started with my companions for Zeeland and Sebastian Imhof lent me 5 fl. The first night we lay at anchor in the sea; it was very cold and we had neither food nor drink. On Saturday we came to Goes, and there I drew a girl in her costume. Thence we went to Arnemuiden and I paid 15 st. for expenses. We passed by a sunken place, and saw the tops of the roofs standing up out of the water. And we went by the little island Wolfersdyk and past the little town Kort-

Stephan Capelle. Stefan Capello of Malines, goldsmith to the Regent Marguerite. Dürer drew his portrait in Antwerp. See plate 28.

Felix kneeling. The drawing is in the Albertina in Vienna. See Plate 67.

Herr Lazarus. Lazarus of Ravensburg, agent in Portugal of the Hochstätters.

Bergen. The town of Bergen-op-Zoom in North Brabant.

Jan de Has. Dürer's host in Bergen.

The old woman. The drawing is in the Musée Condé in Chantilly. See Plate 9.

The von Bergen house. The Palace of the Marquis of Bergen-op-Zoom, the *Markiezenhof*. A view of Bergen from Dürer's Sketchbook is in the Musée Condé in Chantilly. See Plate 8.

A girl. See Plate 10.

A sunken place. The villages of Zeeland frequently suffered floods.

gene on another island lying near. Zeeland has seven islands, and Arnemuiden, where I spent the night, is the largest. From thence I went to Middelburg. There, in the Abbey, is a great picture painted by Jan de Mabuse—not so good in the modelling as in the colouring. I went next to the Veere, where lie ships from all lands; it is a very fine little town.

At Arnemuiden, where I landed before, a great misfortune befel me. As we were pushing ashore and getting out our rope, a great ship bumped hard against us, as we were in the act of landing, and in the crush I had let every one get out before me, so that only I, Georg Kötzler, two old wives, and the skipper with a small boy were left in the ship. When now the other ship bumped against us, and I with those named was still in the ship and could not get out, the strong rope broke; and thereupon, in the same moment, a storm of wind arose, which drove our ship back with force. Then we all cried for help but no one would risk himself for us. And the wind carried us away out to sea. Thereupon the skipper tore his hair and cried aloud, for all his men had landed and the ship was unmanned. Then were we in fear and danger, for the wind was strong and only six persons in the ship. So I spoke to the skipper that he should take courage and have hope in God, and that he should consider what was to be done. So he said that if he could haul up the small sail he would try if we could come again to land. So we toiled all together and got it feebly about half-way up, and went on again towards the land. And when the people on shore, who had already given us up, saw how we helped ourselves, they came to our aid and we got to land.

Middelburg is a good town; it has a very beautiful Townhall with a fine tower. There is much art shown in all things here. In the Abbey the stalls are very costly and beautiful, and there is a splendid gallery of stone; and there is a fine Parish Church.

Jan de Mabuse. The painter Jan Gossaert of Mabuse (1470-1541). The painting, a Descent from the Cross, was destroyed by fire in 1568.

Georg Kötzler. A citizen of Nuremberg (1471-1529).

Townhall. Built by Rombout Keldermans in 1512.

Abbey. The Premonstratensian Abbey in Middelburg.

The town was besides excellent for sketching. Zeeland is fine and wonderful to see because of the water, for it stands higher than the land. I made a portrait of my host at Arnemuiden. Master Hugo and Alexander Imhof and Friedrich the Hirsch-vogels' servant gave me, each of them, an Indian cocoa-nut which they had won at play and the host gave me a sprouting bulb.

A sprouting bulb. Tulip.

Early on Monday we started again by ship and went by the Veere and Zierikzee and tried to get sight of the great fish, but the tide had carried him off again. I paid 2 fl. for fare and expenses and 2 fl. for a rug, 4 st. for a fig-cheese, and 3 st. for carriage, and I lost 6 st. at play, and we have come back to Bergen. I bought an ivory comb for 10 st. I have taken Schnabhan's portrait; I have also taken the portrait of the host's son-in-law Klaus. I gave 2 fl. less 5 st. for a piece of tin, also 2 fl. for a bad piece of tin. I have also made the portraits of little Bernard of Bresslen, Georg Kötzler, and the Frenchman from Kamrich; each of them gave me 1 fl. at Bergen. Jan de Has' son-in-law gave 1 Horn fl. for his portrait, and Kerpen of Köln also gave me 1 fl. for his. Further I bought two bed-covers for 4 fl. less 10 st. I took the portrait of Niklas, the jeweller. I have now eaten thus often at Bergen since I came from Zeeland //////////, and once for 4 st. I paid the driver 3 st. and spent 8 st. and came back to Antwerp to Jobst Plankfelt's on Friday after Lucia's, 1520, and for the times I have eaten with him it is paid, and for my wife it is also paid.

Klaus. Son-in-law of Jan de Has.

Bresslen. Breslau or Brussels?

Kerpen of Köln. Bernard of Kerpen, Marshal to the Count of Nassau.

In return for the 3 books which I gave him Herr Lazarus von Ravensburg has given me : a great fish-scale, 5 snail-shells, 4 medals of silver, 5 of copper, 2 little dried fishes, a white coral, 4 cane-arrows, and another white coral. I changed 1 fl. for expenses, likewise changed a crown. I have eaten alone thus often /////////. The Factor of Portugal gave me a brown velvet bag and a box of good electuary; I gave his lad 3 st. errand-money. I paid 1 Horn fl. for two little panels, but they gave me 6 st. back. I bought a little baboon for 4 gold fl. and five fish for 14 st. I have paid Jobst 10 st. for three dinners. I paid 2 st. for 2 tracts. I gave the messenger 2 st. I gave Lazarus Ravensburger a portrait head on a panel, which cost 6 st.; and besides that I gave him 8 of the large engravings, 8 of the half-sheets, an engraved Passion, and other engravings and wood-cuts, worth altogether more than 4 fl. Further, I have changed 1 Philips fl. for expenses and again I have changed a gold fl. for expenses. I bought a panel for 6 st. and drew the portrait of the servant of the Portuguese on it in charcoal, all which I gave him for a New Year's gift and 2 st. for "trinkgeld". I have changed 1 fl. for expenses, and given Bernhard Stecher a whole set of prints. Bought 31 st. worth of wood. I took portraits of Gerhard Bombelli and the daughter of Sebastian the Procurator. I have changed 1 fl. for expenses. I spent 3 st.; again paid 3 st. for a meal. I gave Herr Wolf von Rogendorf a "Passion" in copper and one in woodcut. Ger-hard Bombelli gave me a printed Turkish cloth and Herr Wolf von Rogendorf gave me 7 Brabant ells of velvet, so I gave his man 1 Philips fl. for "trinkgeld". I paid 3 st. for a meal. I gave 4 st. for a "trinkgeld". I have taken the new Factor's portrait in charcoal. I bought a little tablet for 6 st. I have dined with the Portuguese thus often ////////, with the Treasurer /, with Tomasin ////////// (I gave 4 st. for "trinkgeld"), with Lazarus Ravensburger /, Wolf von Rogendorf /, Bernhard Stecher /, Utz Hanolt Meyting /, Caspar Lewenter /. I gave 3 st. to the man whose portrait I drew. Further I gave the lad 2 st. I paid 4 fl. for flax. I have received 4 fl. for prints. I changed a crown for expenses. I paid the skinner 4 st., further 2 st. I lost 4 st. at play and spent 6 st. I changed a

Daughter of Sebastian. The "beautiful, young lady", fiancée of Gerhard Bombelli. Dürer drew her portrait in his Sketch-book. See Plate 12.

Coat-of-arms with three lion's heads.

New Factor. Rodrigo Fernandez d'Almada (see above). The drawing is in the Berlin Print Room. See Plate 49.

Treasurer. Lorenz Sterck (see above).

3 st. to the man. Probably the old man of ninety-three years who served as the model for the painting of Saint Jerome in prayer. See Plates 43 and 44.

rose-noble for expenses. I bought raisins and 3 pairs of knives for 18 st. I paid 2 fl. for some meals at Jobst's. I lost 4 st. at play and gave 6 st. to the skinner. I gave Master Jakob two engraved "Jeromes". Again lost 2 st. at play. I changed a crown for expenses. I played away 1 st. I gave three pair of knives to Tomasin's three maids; they cost 5 st. I have received 29 st. for prints.

Rodrigo gave me a musk-ball as it had been cut from the Musk-deer, also a quarter of a pound of Persio-paint, besides a box full of quince electuary, and a great box full of sugar; so I gave his lad 5 st. for "trinkgeld". Lost 2 st. at play. I drew a portrait of Jobst's wife in charcoal. I have been paid 4 fl. 5 st. for 3 watercolour drawings on small cloths. Exchanged 2 fl. in succession for expenses. I lost 2 st. at play. My wife gave 1 fl. for the child, and 4 st. at the childbed. I have changed a crown for expenses and spent 4 st.; lost 2 st. at play; gave the messenger 4 st. I changed 1 fl. for expenses. I gave Master Dietrich, the glass-painter, an "Apocalypse" and the 6 "Knots". I paid 40 st. for flax. I lost 8 st. at play. To the little Factor of Portugal, Signor Francisco, I gave my little cloth with the young "Child", it is worth 10 fl. I gave Dr Loffen at Antwerp the 4 "Books" and an engraved "Jerome". I drew the arms of Jobst Plankfelt, Staiber, and another. I have drawn with the metal-point the portraits of Tomasin's son and daughter; also painted a Duke's likeness in oils on a small panel. I have been paid 5 st. for prints. Rodrigo, the Portuguese secretary gave me two Calicut cloths, one of them silk, and gave me an ornamented cap, a green jug with Myrobalans, and a branch of a cedar tree, worth 10 fl. altogether; and I gave the lad 5 st. for "trinkgeld". Paid besides 2 st. for a brush. I made the Fuggers' people a drawing for a masque and they gave me an angel. I changed 1 fl. for expenses. I

Master Jakob. Jacob of Lübeck, painter to the Rogendorfs.

Persio-paint. The meaning is not clear.

Master Dietrich. The glass-painter Dirck J. Vellert.

Francisco. Francisco Pesão (see above).

Young Child. A *putto*.

Doctor Loffen. Physician to the Emperor Maximilian.

Coat-of-arms of Lorenz Staiber.

Duke's likeness. A figure of a Roman in armour called by the Humanists "*dux*".

Myrobalans. A species of Indian fruit possessing curative qualities.

An angel. An old English gold coin.

paid 8 st. for two little powder-horns. 3 st. I lost at play. I changed an angel for expenses. I have drawn Tomasin two sheets-full of very fine little masks. I painted a good "Veronica Face" in oils; it is worth 12 fl. I gave it to Francisco, Factor of Portugal. Then I painted another "Veronica Face" in oils, a better one than the former, and I gave it to Factor Brandão of Portugal. Francisco first gave the maid 1 Philips fl. "trinkgeld" but afterwards because of the "Veronica" he gave her 1 fl. more; Factor Brandão also gave her 1 fl. I paid Peter 8 st. for two cases. I have changed an angel for expenses.

On Carnival Sunday the goldsmiths invited me to dinner early with my wife. Amongst their assembled guests were many notable men. They had prepared a most splendid meal and did me exceeding great honour. And in the evening the

The old Bailiff. Gerard van de Werve, a Knight.

old Bailiff of the town invited me and gave a splendid meal and did me great honour. Many strange masquers came there.

Flores. Fleurequin Neefs.

I have drawn the portrait in charcoal of Flores, Lady Margaret's organist. On Monday night Herr Lopez invited me

Herr Lopes. Thomas Lopes, Portuguese Ambassador, once Portuguese Factor in Antwerp.

to the great banquet on Shrove-Tuesday which lasted till 2 o'clock and was very costly. Herr Lorenz Sterck gave me a Spanish fur. To the above-mentioned feast very many came in costly masks and especially Tomasin and Brandão. I won 2 fl. at play. I bought a basket of raisins for 14 st. I took the portrait in charcoal of Bernhard von Castell, the man from whom I won the money. Tomasin's brother Gerhard gave me 4 Brabant ells of the best black satin, and 3 large boxes of candied citron, so I gave the maid 3 st. for "trinkgeld". I paid 13 st. for wood and 2 st. for varnish. I drew with the metalpoint a careful portrait of the Procurator's daughter. I changed 1 angel for expenses. I took a portrait in black chalk of the

Master Jean. Jean Mone, sculptor from Lorraine, recorded in Brussels in 1536.

good marble sculptor Master Jean, who is like Christoph

Coler. He has studied in Italy and comes from Metz. I changed 1 Horn fl. for expenses. I gave Jan Türck 3 fl. for Italian art-wares, and I gave him 12 ducats' worth of prints for an ounce of good ultramarine. I sold a small woodcut "Passion" for 3 fl. I sold 2 sketches and 4 books of Schäufelein's prints for 3 fl. I bought two ivory saltcellars from Calicut for 3 fl. I have been paid 2 fl. for prints. I changed 1 fl. for expenses. Rüdiger von Gelern gave me a snail-shell and coins of gold and silver—together worth 1/4 fl. I gave him in return 3 Large Books and an engraved "Knight". I have been paid 11 st. for prints. I bought the "SS. Peter and Paul", which I mean to give to Coler's wife, for 2 Philips fl. Rodrigo gave me again 2 boxes of quince electuary and many sweetmeats of all kinds, and I gave 5 st. for "trinkgeld". I paid 16 st. for boxes. Lazarus Ravensburger gave me a sugarloaf, so I gave his lad 1 st. I paid 6 st. for wood. I dined once with the Frenchman, twice with the Hirschvogels' Fritz, and once with Master Peter Aegidius the Secretary, when Erasmus of Rotterdam also dined with us.

I paid 1 st. to be allowed to go up the tower at Antwerp; it is said to be higher than the one at Strassburg. I looked from it over the whole town on all sides, which was very pleasant. I paid 1 st. for a bath. I changed 1 angel for expenses. Brandão Factor of Portugal, gave me 2 fine large white sugar-loaves, a dish-full of sweetmeats, 2 green pots of preserves, and 4 ells of black satin, so I gave the servants 10 st. for "trinkgeld". I paid the messenger 3 st. I have twice more drawn with the metal-point the portrait of the beautiful maiden for Gerhard. I again changed an angel for expenses. I received 4 fl. for art-wares. I paid 10 st. for Rodrigo's case. I dined with the Treasurer, Herr Lorenz Sterck; he gave me an ivory whistle and a very pretty piece of porcelain, so I gave him a

Christoph Coler. A citizen of Nuremberg (1483-1536).

Jan Türck. Painter and picture merchant, Jacob Tierik (died 1567).

Schäufelein's prints. The works of Dürer's pupil Hans Leonhard Schäufelein (1490-1540).

Rüdiger von Gelern. Of Gelderland?

Frenchman. Possibly the "Frenchman from Kamrich" whom Dürer met in Zeeland, or the French sculptor Jean Mone (see above).

Master Peter Aegidius. Petrus Aegidius, a friend of Erasmus of Rotterdam (1486-1553).

Rodrigo's case. For Rodrigo d'Almada's painting.

Herr Adrian. Adriaen Herbouts, advocate to the town (died 1546).

Guild of merchants. This was the Guild of Mercers, whose headquarters, "*In den Zwarten Arend*", was situated in the Grand-Place. The payment is recorded in their accounts.

whole set of prints. I also gave a whole set to Herr Adrian, public orator of Antwerp. I changed a Philips fl. for expenses. I presented a "S. Nicholas sitting" to the largest and richest guild of merchants at Antwerp. They gave me 3 Philips fl. for it. I gave Peter the old frame of the "S. Jerome" and 4 fl. besides for a frame for the Treasurer's likeness. I paid 11 st. for wood. I again changed a Philips fl. for expenses and bought a gimlet for 4 st. I gave 3 st. for 3 canes.

I have handed my bale over to Jacob and Andreas Hessler to take to Nürnberg and I am to pay them 2 fl. per cwt. of Nürnberg weight. They are to take it to Herr Hans Imhof the elder, and I paid them 2 fl. on it, I also packed it in a packing case—this was in the year 1521 on the Sunday before "Judicae".

On Saturday before Judicae Rodrigo gave me 6 large Indian cocoa-nuts, a very fine stem of coral, and 2 large Portuguese fl. one weighing 10 ducats, and I gave his man 15 st. for "trinkgeld". Also I bought a load-stone for 16 st. Further I changed 1 angel for expenses. I paid 6 st. for packing. I sent Master Hugo at Brussels an engraved Passion and some other prints in return for his little porphyry stone. I made Tomasin a design, drawn and tinted in half colours, after which he intends to have his house painted. I painted a "Jerome" carefully in oils and gave it to Rodrigo of Portugal; he gave Susanna a ducat for "trinkgeld". I changed 1 Philips fl. for expenses and gave 10 st. to my father-confessor. I paid 4 st. for the little tortoise. I dined with Herr Gilbert, and he gave me a small Calicut "target" made of a fish-skin, and two gloves with which the natives there fight. I paid Peter 2 st. I gave 10 st. for the fish-fins, and gave 3 st. for "trinkgeld". I have made a very good portrait in hard chalk of Cornelius the Secretary to the Magistrates of Antwerp. I bought the five silk girdles, which I mean to give away, for 3 fl. 16 st.;

S. Jerome. The painting is in Lisbon Museum. See Plate I, p. 25.

Cornelius. Cornelis Grapheus, secretary to the Town of Antwerp (1482-1558).

also a border ("Borte") for 20 st. These 6 borders I sent to the wives of Caspar Nützel, Hans Imhof, Sträub, the two Spenglers, and Loffelholz, and to each a good pair of gloves. To Pirkheimer I sent a large cap, a costly inkstand of buffalo-horn, a silver Emperor, 1 pound of pistachios, and 3 sugar canes. To Caspar Nützel I sent a great elk's foot, 10 large fircones, and cones of the stone-pine. To Jacob Muffel I sent a scarlet breast-cloth of one ell; to Hans Imhof's child an embroidered scarlet cap and stone-pine nuts; to Kramer's wife 4 ells of silk worth 4 fl.; to Lochinger's wife 1 ell of silk worth 1 fl.; to the two Spenglers a bag and 3 fine horns each; to Herr Hieronymus Holzschuher a very large horn. I have dined twice with the Factor.

I dined with Master Adrian, Secretary to the Council of Antwerp, and he gave me the small panel painted by Master Joachim, it represents "Lot with his Daughters". I again received 12 fl. for art-wares. I also sold some of Hans Grün's works for 1 fl. Rüdiger von Gelern gave me a piece of sandalwood; I gave his lad 1 st. I painted Bernhard von Resten's portrait in oils, for which he paid me 8 fl., and gave my wife a crown, and Susanna a florin worth 24 st. I gave 3 st. for the Swiss jug and 2 st. for the boat, also 3 st. for the case, and 4 st. to the father-confessor. I changed an angel for expenses. I received 4 fl. 10 st. for art-wares. I paid 3 st. for salve. I paid 12 half-stivers for wood. I changed 1 fl. for expenses. I bought 14 pieces of French wood for 1 fl. I gave Ambrosius Hochstetter a "Life of Our Lady", and he gave me a sketch of his ship. Rodrigo gave my wife a little ring which is worth more than 5 fl. I changed 1 fl. for expenses. I have drawn the portrait in charcoal of Factor Brandão's Secretary. I drew with the metal-point a portrait of his Moorish servant, and one of Rodrigo with the pencil in black and white on a large

To each. All members of Nuremberg patrician families.

Pirkheimer. Willibald Pirckheimer, Burgomaster of Nuremberg (1470-1530).

Caspar Nützel. Burgomaster of Nuremberg (1471-1529).

Jacob Muffel. Burgomaster of Nuremberg (1471-1526). Dürer made his portrait in 1526.

Hieronymus Holzschuher Burgomaster of Nuremberg (1469-1529). Dürer made his portrait in 1526.

Master Adrian. Adriaen Herbouts (see above).

Master Joachim. The painter Joachim Patinir (see above).

Hans Grün. The painter Hans Baldung Grien (1485-1545).

Bernhard von Resten. The portrait is in Dresden Museum. A drawing in charcoal of the same person is in the British Museum. See Plate II, p. 33.

The boat. A gift from Hochstetter.

The case. Intended for Hochstetter's portrait.

French wood. A remedy against venereal disease.

Ambrosius Hochstetter. An Augsburg merchant, settled in Antwerp in 1485. He went bankrupt in 1529 and died in prison in 1534.

Portrait of his Moorish servant. The drawing is in the Uffizi in Florence. The servant's name was Catherina; she was 18 years of age. See Plate 66.

Rodrigo. See Plate 49.

piece of paper. I paid 16 fl. for a piece of camlet which measured 24 ells and cost 1 st. to bring home. For gloves I paid 2 st. I took the portrait of Lukas of Danzig in charcoal, and he paid me 1 fl. for it and gave me a piece of sandalwood.

On Saturday after Easter I set off from Antwerp by the Scheldt for Bruges with Hans Lieber and Master Jan Prost, a good painter born at Bruges, and we came to Beveren, a large village, and thence to another large village Vracene. After that we passed thro' some hamlets and came to a fine large village where the rich farmers live, and there we breakfasted. We then passed the rich Abbey of S. Paul, and went through Caudenborn, a beautiful village, and after that thro' the large, long village of Kalve, and thence to Ertvelde. We stayed the night there, and on Sunday we were up betimes and went on from Ertvelde to a little town and from it we went to Ecloo. Ecloo is a mighty large village, it is plastered and has a square; there we breakfasted. We went on thence to Maldegem, and then thro' other villages and came to Bruges—a noble and beautiful town. I paid 21 st. for fare and other expenses.

When I reached Bruges Jan Prost took me in to lodge in his house and prepared the same night a costly meal and bade much company to meet me. Next day Marx, the goldsmith, invited me and gave me a costly meal and asked many to meet me. Afterwards they took me to see the Emperor's house which is large and splendid. I saw the chapel there which Roger painted, and some pictures by a great old master; I gave 1 st. to the man who showed us them. Then I bought 3 ivory combs for 30 st. They took me next to S. Jacob's and showed me the precious pictures by Roger and Hugo, who were both great masters. Then I saw in Our Lady's Church the alabaster Virgin, sculptured by Michelangelo of Rome. After that they took me to many more churches

Hans Lieber. Of an Augsburg patrician family (died 1554).

Jan Prost. Jan Prevost (see above).

Marx. Marc de Glasere (see above).

The Emperor's house. The Prinsenhof, built by the Dukes of Burgundy.

The chapel. Probably refers to a mural painting.

Roger and Hugo. The painters Roger van der Weyden (c. 1400-1464) and Hugo van der Goes (died 1482).

The alabaster Virgin. The statue is still in the place where Dürer saw it.

and showed me all the good pictures, of which there is an abundance there; and when I had seen the Jan and all the other works, we came at last to the painters' chapel, in which there are good things. Then they prepared a banquet for me, and I went with them from it to their guild-hall, where many honourable men were gathered together, both goldsmiths, painters and merchants, and they made me sup with them. They gave me presents, sought to make my acquaintance, and did me great honour. The two brothers Jacob and Peter Mostaert, the councillors, gave me 12 cans of wine; and the whole assembly, more than 60 persons, accompanied me home with many torches. I also saw at their shooting court the great fish-tub on which they eat; it is 19 feet long, 7 feet high, and 7 feet wide.

So early on Tuesday we went away, but before that I drew with the metal-point the portrait of Jan Prost, and gave his wife 10 st. at parting. From Bruges we travelled to Ursel, and breakfasted there; on the way there are three villages. Thence we went on through three villages more to Ghent and I paid 4 st. for the journey and 4 st. for other expenses.

On my arrival at Ghent the Dean of the Painters came to me and brought with him the first masters in painting; they showed me great honour, received me most courteously, offered me their goodwill and service, and supped with me. On Wednesday they took me early to the Beffroi of S. John whence I looked over the great wonderful town, yet in which even I had just been taken for something great. Then I saw Jan's picture; it is a most precious painting, full of thought, and the Eve, Mary, and God the Father are specially good. Next I saw the lions and drew one with metal-point. And I saw at the place where men are beheaded on the bridge, the two statues erected as a sign that there a son beheaded his

Jan. The painter Jan van Eyck (died 1441).

Painters' chapel. Built in 1450 and situated on Noordzandstraat. The only painting from the collection that still exists is the portrait of Jan van Eyck's wife.

Shooting court. It still exists on the Karmelietenstraat.

Beffroi of S. John. The tower of the church of Saint-Bavon, originally dedicated to Saint John the Baptist.

Jan's picture. Jan van Eyck's "Adoration of the Lamb", still in the church of Saint-Bavon.

The lions. The drawings are in the Albertina, Vienna and the Berlin Print Room. See Plates 18 and 19.

The bridge. The Hoofdbrug, adorned with the two statues (built 1371).

father. Ghent is a fine and remarkable town; four great waters flow through it. I gave the sacristan and the lions' keepers 3 st. "trinkgeld". I saw many wonderful things in Ghent besides, and the painters with their Dean did not leave me alone, but they are with me morning and evening and paid for everything and were very friendly to me. I gave away 5 st. at the inn at leaving.

So early on Thursday I set out from Ghent and passed through some villages to the inn called the Swan, where we breakfasted. Then we went on thro' a fine village and came to Antwerp and the fare was 8 st.

I have received 4 fl. for art-wares. I changed 1 fl. for expenses. I took the portrait of Hans Lieber of Ulm in charcoal; he wanted to pay me 1 fl. but I would not take it. I gave 7 st. for wood and 1 st. for bringing it. I changed 1 fl. for expenses. In the third week after Easter a violent fever seized me, with great weakness, nausea, and headache. And before, when I was in Zeeland, a wondrous sickness overcame me, such as I never heard of from any man, and this sickness remains with me. I paid 6 st. for cases. The monk has bound 2 books for me in return for the art-wares which I gave him. I bought a piece of Arras to make two mantles for my mother-in-law and my wife, for 10 fl. 8 st. I paid the Doctor 8 st. and 3 st. to the apothecary. I also changed 1 fl. for expenses, and spent 3 st. in company. Paid the Doctor 10 st. I again paid the Doctor 6 st. During my illness Rodrigo has sent me many sweetmeats. I gave the lad 4 st. "trinkgeld". I have drawn with the metal-point the portrait of Master Joachim and made him besides another likeness with the metal-point. I changed a crown for expenses. I again changed 1 fl. for expenses. Paid the Doctor 6 st., also 7 st. at the apothecary's. 1 fl. I changed for expenses.

For packing the third bale, which I sent from Antwerp to Nürn-

Master Joachim. The painter Joachim Patinir (see above). Some writers have suggested that the charcoal drawing originally in the Schlossmuseum in Weimar represents Patinir. See Plate 56.

berg by a carrier, named Hans Staber, I paid 13 st.; and I paid the carrier 1 fl. for it, and agreed with him to take it from Antwerp to Nürnberg for 1 1/4 fl. the hundredweight. This bale too is to be taken to Hans Imhof the elder. I paid the Doctor, the apothecary, and the barber 14 st. I gave Master Jacob, the surgeon, 4 fl. worth of prints. I have taken in charcoal the portrait of Thomas Bologna of Rome. My camlet coat came to 21 Brabant ells, which are 3 finger-breadths longer than Nürnberg ells. Also I bought black Spanish skins for it which cost 3 st. each, and there are 34 of them, makes 10 fl. 2 st.; then I paid the skinner 1 fl. for making them up; further there came 2 ells of velvet for trimming—5 fl.; also for silk, cord, and thread 34 st.; then the tailor's wage 30 st.; the camlet in the coat cost 14 fl. 1 st.; also 5 st."trinkgeld" for the lad.

Thomas Bologna. Tommaso Vincidor of Bologna (see above).

Cantate Sunday after Easter—from this I start a fresh account. I have again paid the Doctor 6 st. I received 53 st. for artwares and took them for expenses.

On Sunday after Rogation week Master Joachim, the good landscape painter, asked me to his wedding and showed me all honour. And I saw two fine plays there and the first was especially pious and devout. I again paid the Doctor 6 st. I changed 1 fl. for expenses.

On Sunday after Our Lord's Ascension-day Master Dietrich, the Antwerp glasspainter, invited me and asked many others to meet me; and amongst them especially Alexander the goldsmith, a rich, stately man, and we had a costly feast and they did me great honour. I made the portrait in charcoal of Master Marx, the goldsmith who lives at Bruges. I bought a broad cap for 36 st. I paid Paul Geiger 1 fl. to take my little box to Nürnberg and 4 st. for the letter. I took the portrait of Ambrosius Hochstetter in charcoal and dined with him. I have also eaten with Tomasin at least six times. I bought some

Paul Geiger. Nuremberg merchant.

wooden dishes and platters for 3 st.   I paid the apothecary 12 st.
I gave away two copies of the "Life of Our Lady"—the one to
the foreign surgeon, the other to Marx's house-servant.
I also paid the Doctor 8 st.   I paid 4 st. for cleaning an old cap,
lost 4 st. at play.   I paid 2 fl. for a new cap, and have exchanged
the first cap, because it was clumsy, and added 6 st. more for
another.   I have painted the portrait of a Duke in oils.   I have
made a very fine and careful portrait in oils of the Treasurer

Lorenz Sterck. See Pl. III, p. 45.

Lorenz Sterck; it was worth 25 fl.   I presented it to him and
in return he gave me 20 fl. and Susanna 1 fl. "trinkgeld".   Likewise painted the portrait of Jobst my host very finely and carefully in oils. He has now given me his for his. And his wife have
I done again and made her portrait in oils.

On Friday before Whitsunday in the year 1521, came tidings
to me at Antwerp, that Martin Luther had been so treacherously taken prisoner; for he trusted the Emperor Charles,
who had granted him his herald and imperial safe-conduct.
But as soon as the herald had conveyed him to an unfriendly
place near Eisenach he rode away, saying that he no longer
needed him.   Straightway there appeared ten knights and they
treacherously carried off the pious man, betrayed into their
hands, a man enlightened by the Holy Ghost, a follower of the
true Christian faith.   And whether he yet lives I know not, or
whether they have put him to death; if so, he has suffered for
the truth of Christ and because he rebuked the unchristian
Papacy, which strives with its heavy load of human laws against
the redemption of Christ.   And if he has suffered it is that we
may again be robbed and stripped of the fruit of our blood and
sweat, that the same may be shamefully and scandalously
squandered by idle-going folk, while the poor and the sick
therefore die of hunger.   But this is above all most grievous
to me, that, may be, God will suffer us to remain still longer

under their false, blind doctrine, invented and drawn up by the men alone whom they call Fathers, by whom also the precious Word of God is in many places wrongly expounded or utterly ignored. Oh God of heaven pity us! Oh Lord Jesus Christ pray for Thy people! Deliver us at the fit time. Call together Thy far-scattered sheep by Thy voice in the Scripture, called thy godly Word. Help us to know this Thy voice and to follow no other deceiving cry of human error, so that we, Lord Jesus Christ, may not fall away from Thee. Call together again the sheep of Thy pasture, who are still in part found in the Roman Church, and with them also the Indians, Muscovites, Russians, and Greeks, who have been scattered by the oppression and avarice of the Pope and by false appearance of holiness. Oh God, redeem Thy poor people constrained by heavy bann and edict, which it nowise willingly obeys, continually to sin against its conscience if it disobeys them. Never, oh God, hast Thou so horribly burdened a people with human laws as us poor folk under the Roman chair, who daily long to be free Christians, ransomed by Thy blood. Oh highest, heavenly Father, pour into our hearts, through Thy Son, Jesus Christ, such a light, that by it we may know what messenger we are bound to obey, so that with good conscience we may lay aside the burdens of others and serve Thee, eternal, heavenly Father, with happy and joyful hearts. And if we have lost this man, who has written more clearly than any that has lived for 140 years, and to whom Thou hast given such a spirit of the Gospel, we pray Thee, oh heavenly Father, that Thou wouldst again give Thy Holy Spirit to one, that he may gather anew everywhere together Thy Holy Christian Church, that we may again live free and in Christian manner, and so, by our good works, all unbelievers, as Turks, Heathen, and Calicuts, may of themselves turn to us and embrace the Christian faith. But,

Than any that has lived for 140 years. Dürer probably refers to John Wycliffe (died 1384).

'ere thou judgest, oh Lord, Thou willest that, as Thy Son, Jesus Christ, was fain to die by the hands of the priests, and to rise from the dead and after to ascend up to heaven, so too in like manner it should be with Thy follower Martin Luther, whose life the Pope compasseth with his money, treacherously towards God. Him wilt thou quicken again. And as thou, oh my Lord, ordainest thereafter that Jerusalem should for that sin be destroyed, so wilt thou also destroy this self-assumed authority of the Roman Chair. Oh Lord, give us then the new beautified Jerusalem, which descendeth out of heaven, whereof the Apocalypse writes, the holy, pure Gospel, which is not obscured by human doctrine. Every man who reads Martin Luther's books may see how clear and transparent is his doctrine, because he sets forth the holy Gospel. Wherefore his books are to be held in great honour and not to be burnt; unless indeed his adversaries, who ever strive against the truth and would make gods out of men, were also cast into the fire, they and all their opinions with them, and afterwards a new edition of Luther's works were prepared. Oh God, if Luther be dead, who will henceforth expound to us the holy Gospel with such clearness? What, oh God, might he not still have written for us in ten or twenty years! Oh all ye pious Christian men, help me deeply to bewail this man, inspired of God, and to pray Him yet again to send us an enlightened man. Oh Erasmus of Rotterdam, where wilt thou stop? Behold how the wicked tyranny of wordly power, the might of darkness, prevails. Hear, thou knight of Christ! Ride on by the side of the Lord Jesus. Guard the truth. Attain the martyr's crown. Already indeed art thou an aged little man ("ein altes Männiken"), and myself have heard thee say that thou givest thyself but two years more wherein thou mayest still be fit to accomplish somewhat. Lay out the same well for the good of the Gospel and of the true Christian faith, and make thyself heard. So, as Christ says, shall the Gates of Hell (the Roman Chair) in no wise prevail against thee. And if here below thou wert to be like thy master Christ and sufferedst infamy at the hands of the liars of this time, and didst die a little the sooner, then wouldst thou the sooner pass from death unto life and be glorified in Christ. For if thou drinkest of the cup which He drank of, with Him shalt thou reign and judge with justice those who have dealt unrighteously. Oh Erasmus, cleave to this that God himself may be thy praise, even as it is written of David. For thou mayest, yea verily thou mayest overthrow Goliath. Because God stands by the Holy Christian Church, even as He only upholds the Roman Church, according to His godly will. May He help us to everlasting salvation, who is God, the Father, the Son, and Holy Ghost, one eternal God! Amen. Oh ye Christian men, pray God for help, for His judgment draweth nigh and His justice shall appear. Then shall we behold the innocent blood which the Pope, Priests, Bishops, and Monks have shed, judged and condemned ("Apocal."). These are the slain who lie beneath the Altar of God and cry for vengeance, to whom the voice of God answereth: Await the full number of the innocent slain, then will I judge.

I again changed 1 fl. for expenses. I paid the Doctor 8 st. I have dined twice with Rodrigo. I dined with the rich Canon. I changed 1 fl. for expenses. I had Master Konrad, the Mechlin sculptor, for my guest on Whitsunday. I paid 18 st. for Italian prints. Again 6 st. for the Doctor. For Master Joachim have I drawn 4 small St Christophers on grey paper.

On the last day of Whitsuntide I was at the great horse-fair at Antwerp and there I saw a great number of fine stallions ridden, and two stallions in particular were sold for 700 fl. I have been paid 1 3/4 fl. for prints, the money I used for expenses; paid

Master Konrad. Konrad Meit, sculptor to the Regent Marguerite.

St Christophers. In the Berlin Print Room are nine sketches in pen made in connection with the four drawings. See Plates 48 and 90.

the Doctor 4 st. I bought two little books for 3 st. 3 times have I dined with Tomasin. I designed 3 swords-hilts for him and he gave me a small alabaster bowl. I took an English nobleman's portrait in charcoal and he gave me 1 fl. which I changed for expenses. Master Gerhard, the illuminator, has a daughter about 18 years old named Susanna. She has illuminated a "Salvator" on a little sheet, for which I gave her 1 fl. It is very wonderful that a woman can do so much. I lost 6 st. at play.

I saw the great Procession at Antwerp on Holy Trinity day. Master Konrad gave me a fine pair of knives, so I gave his little old man a Life of Our Lady in return. I have made a portrait in charcoal of Master Jan, goldsmith of Brussels, also one of his wife. I have been paid 2 fl. for prints. Master Jan, the Brussels goldsmith, paid me 3 Philips fl. for what I did for him, the drawing for the seal and the two portraits. I gave the "Veronica", which I painted in oils, and the "Adam and Eve" which Franz did, to Jan the goldsmith in exchange for a jacinth and an agate, on which a Lucretia is engraved. Each of us valued his portion at 14 fl. Further I gave him a whole set of engravings for a ring and 6 stones. Each valued his portion at 7 fl. I bought 2 pairs of shoes for 14 st. and two small boxes for 2 st. I changed 2 Philips fl. for expenses. I drew 3 "Leadings-forth" and 2 "Mounts of Olives" on 5 half-sheets. I took 3 portraits in black and white on grey paper. I also sketched in black and white on grey paper two Netherland costumes. I painted for the Englishman his coat-of-arms and he gave me 1 fl. I have also at one time and another done many drawings and other things to serve different people, and for the more part of my work have received nothing. Andreas of Krakau paid me 1 Philips fl. for a shield and a Child's head. Changed 1 fl. for expenses. I paid 2 fl. for sweeping-brushes.

I saw the great Procession at Antwerp on Corpus Christi day, it was very splendid. I gave 4 st. as "trinkgeld". I paid the Doctor 6 st. and 1 st. for a box. I have dined 5 times with Tomasin. I paid 10 st. at the apothecary's and gave his wife 14 st. for the clyster and himself 15 st. for the prescription. I again changed 2 Philips fl. for expenses. Further I paid the Doctor 6 st. I again paid the apothecary's wife 10 st. for the clyster, and 4 st. at the shop. To the monk who confessed my wife I gave 8 st. I bought a whole piece of Harras for 8 fl., and about 14 ells of fine Harras for 8 fl. I again paid the apothecary 32 st. for physic. I paid the messenger 3 st., and the tailor 4 st. I dined once with Hans Fehle and thrice with Tomasin. I gave 10 st. for a birthday present.

On the Wednesday after Corpus Christi in the year 1521, I gave over my great bale at Antwerp to a carrier, called by the name Kunz Metz von Schlaudersdorf, to take it to Nürnberg; and I am to pay him for the carrying of it to Nürnberg for every hundredweight 1 1/2 fl. And I paid him 1 fl. on it. And he is to answer for it to Herr Hans Imhof the elder. I drew a portrait in charcoal of young Jakob Rehlinger at Antwerp. I have again dined thrice with Tomasin. On the eighth day after Corpus Christi I went with my people to Lady Margaret at Mechlin. Took 5 st. with me for expenses. My wife changed 1 fl. for expenses. At Mechlin I lodged with Master Heinrich, the painter, at the sign of the Golden Head. And the painters and sculptors bade me as guest at my inn and did me great honour in their gathering. I went also to Poppenreuter the gunmaker's house, and found wonderful things there. And I went to Lady Margaret's and showed her my "Emperor", and would have presented it to her, but she so disliked it that I took it away with me. And on Friday Lady Margaret showed me all her beautiful things; amongst them I saw about 40 small oil pictures, the like of which for

Master Heinrich. Hendrik Kelderman, painter and innkeeper of Malines.

Poppenreuter. Cannon-founder for Charles V (died Malines 1534).

Wonderful things. A drawing of a mortar was in Bremen Museum. See Plate 25.

My "Emperor". Dürer's portrait of Emperor Maximilian, now in Vienna.

40 small oil pictures. The greater part of this series of paintings by Juan de Flandes is in the Royal Palace in Madrid.

Jan. Jan van Eyck. His portrait of Arnolfini and his wife, in the National Gallery, was at the time in the collection of the Regent Marguerite.

Jacob Walch. Jacopo de'Barbari, painter in the service of the Regent Marguerite, in whose collection were many of his works. He had died by 1515.

Her painter. Bernard van Orley (c. 1488-1541).

Library. The famous Burgundian library.

Master Konrad. The sculptor Konrad Meit (see above).

Stephan. Stephen Lullier, Librarian to the Regent Marguerite.

The Augustines. The Augustines of Saxony, settled in Antwerp in 1513, and expelled for heresy in 1523. The monastery was destroyed.

Master Jacob. Probably Jacob Proesten (Jacobus Praepositus), Prior of the Monastery.

Master Lukas. The painter and engraver Lukas van Leyden (1494?-1533).

With the metal-point. The portrait is now in the Museum in Lille. See Plate 65.

Aert Braun. The Dutch painter Aert Bruyn.

precision and excellence I have never beheld. There also I saw more good works by Jan and Jacob Walch. I asked my Lady for Jacob's little book, but she said she had already promised it to her painter. Then I saw many other costly things and a precious library. Master Hans Poppenreuter asked me as his guest. I have had Master Konrad twice and his wife once as my guests. Paid 27 st. and 2 st. for fare. I have also drawn in charcoal portraits of Stephan, the chamberlain, and Master Konrad the figure-carver, and on Saturday I came again from Mechlin to Antwerp.

My trunk started on the Saturday week after Corpus Christi. I have again changed 1 fl. for expenses. Paid the messenger 3 st. I have dined twice with the Augustines. I drew Master Jacob's portrait in charcoal and had a tablet frame made for it—cost 6 st.—and I made him a present of it. I drew portraits of Bernhard Stecher and his wife and gave him a whole set of prints, and I made another portrait of his wife and had a frame made for it for 6 st. All this I gave him, so he gave me 10 fl. in return.

Master Lukas who engraves in copper asked me as his guest. He is a little man, born at Leyden in Holland; he was at Antwerp. I have dined with Master Bernhard Stecher. I paid the messenger 1 1/2 st. I received 4 1/4 fl. for prints.

I have drawn with the metal-point the portrait of Master Lukas van Leyden. I have lost 1 fl. Paid the Doctor 6 st., again 6 st. I gave the Steward of the Augustinian convent at Antwerp a "Life of Our Lady", and 4 st. to his servant. I gave Master Jacob an engraved "Passion" and a woodcut "Passion" and 5 other pieces, and gave 4 st. to his servant. I changed 4 fl. for expenses. I bought 14 fishskins for 2 Philips fl. I have made portraits in black chalk of Aert Braun and his wife. I gave the goldsmith who valued the rings for me 1 fl. worth of prints.

Of the three rings which I took in exchange for prints the two smaller are valued at 15 crowns, but the sapphire is set at 25 crowns—that makes 54 fl. 8 st. And what amongst other things the above Frenchman took was 36 Large Books, makes 9 fl. I bought a screwknife for 2 st. The man with the three rings has overreached me by half. I did not understand the matter. I bought a red cap for my god-child for 18 st. Lost 21 st. at play. Drank 2 st. I bought 3 fine small rubies for 11 gold fl. 12 st. I changed 1 fl. for expenses. I have dined again with the Augustinians. Also I dined twice with Tomasin. I bought 13 porpoise bristle-brushes for 6 st., and 6 bristle-brushes for 3 st.

I made the great Anton Haunolt's portrait in black chalk on a royal-sheet. I made careful portraits in black chalk on two royal-sheets of Aert Braun and his wife, and I drew him once more with the metal-point; he paid me an angel. I again changed 1 fl. for expenses. I bought a pair of boots for 1 fl. I paid 6 st. for a "calamarium". I bought a packing trunk for 12 st. Bought a dozen lady's gloves for 21 st. and a bag for 6 st. and 1. I paid 3 st. for 3 bristle-brushes. I changed 1 fl. for expenses. Gave 1 st. for a piece of morocco leather. Anton Haunolt, whose portrait I took, has given me 3 Philips fl., and Bernard Stecher gave me a tortoise-shell. I made a portrait of his wife's niece, dined once with her husband, and he gave me 2 Philips fl. Gave 1 st. "trinkgeld".

I gave Anton Haunolt 2 Books and received 13 st. for prints. I made Master Joachim a present of Hans Grün's work. Changed 3 Philips fl. for expenses. Have dined twice with Bernhard, also twice with Tomasin. I gave Jobst's wife 4 woodcuts. Gave Friedrich, Jobst's man, 2 Books. I gave glazier Hennik's son 2 Books. Rodrigo gave me one of the parrots which are brought from Malaga, and I gave the servant 5 st. "trinkgeld".

Anton Haunolt. Successor to Bernhard Stecher at the Fuggers' house in Antwerp.

With the metal-point. Possibly the page from Dürer's Sketchbook, with a view of Andernach, in the Berlin Print Room. See Plate 17.

Hans Grün. The German painter Hans Baldung Grien (see above).

Hennik's son. Son of Henne Doghens, a pupil of Vellert, who was received into the Guild of Saint Luke in 1524.

Master Aert. Aert van Ort, received into the Guild of Saint Luke in 1513.

Master Jean. Jean Mone (see above).

Cornelius. Cornelis Grapheus (see above).

Babylonian Captivity. *Von der Babylonischen Gefengknuss der Kirchen.* 1520.

Peter Pot's monk. That is, a monk from Peter Pot's foundation for indigent foreigners.

Two portrait heads. The two portraits mentioned earlier by Dürer.

I have dined twice more with Tomasin. Bought a small cage for 2 st., a pair of long-boots for 3 st., 8 little boards for 4 st. I gave Peter 2 whole-sheet engravings and a woodcut sheet. Have again dined twice with Tomasin. I changed 1 fl. for expenses. I gave Master Aert, the glasspainter, a "Life of Our Lady" and gave Master Jean, the French sculptor, a whole set of prints. He gave my wife 6 very finely made little glasses, full of rose water. Bought a packing-case for 7 st. I changed 1 fl. for expenses, and paid 7 st. for a cut leather bag. Cornelius the Secretary gave me Luther's "Babylonian Captivity", in return for which I gave him my 3 Large Books. I gave Peter Pot's monk 1 fl. worth of prints. To glasspainter Hennik I gave 2 Large Books. I bought a piece of glazed calico for 4 st. I changed 1 Philips fl. for expenses. I gave 8 fl. worth of my prints for a whole set of Lukas' engravings. I again changed 1 Philips fl. for expenses. I bought a bag for 9 st. I gave 7 st. for half-a-dozen Netherlands cards, and 3 st. for a small yellow posthorn. I have paid 24 st. for meat, 12 st. for coarse cloth, and again 5 st. for coarse cloth. I dined twice with Tomasin, gave Peter 1 st. I gave 7 st. for a present, and 3 st. for canvas. Rodrigo gave me 6 ells of rough, black cloth for a mantle, it cost a crown an ell. I changed 2 fl. for expenses. I gave the tailor's man 2 st. for "trinkgeld". I reckoned up with Jobst and found myself 31 fl. in his debt, which I paid him; therein were charged and deducted the two portrait heads which I painted in oils, for which he gave 5 pounds of borax Netherlands' weight. In all my doings, spendings, sales, and other dealings, in all my connexions with high and low, I have suffered loss in the Netherlands; and Lady Margaret in particular gave me nothing for what I made and presented to her. And this settlement with Jobst was made on S. Peter and Paul's day.

I gave Rodrigo's man 7 st. for "trinkgeld". I gave Master Heinrich my engraved "Passion", and he gave me some burning pastilles. I had to pay the tailor 45 st. for making up the mantle. I have engaged with a carrier to take me from Antwerp to Köln. I am to pay him 13 light florins, each worth 24 stivers, and am to pay the expenses of another person and a lad besides. Jacob Rehlinger gave me a ducat for his likeness drawn in charcoal. Gerhard gave me two little casks of capers and olives, for which I gave 4 st. "trinkgeld". I gave Rodrigo's servant 1 st. I exchanged my portrait of the Emperor for a white English cloth which Jacob, Tomasin's son-in-law, gave me. Alexander Imhof has lent me a full 100 gold fl. on the eve of Our Lady's Crossing the Mountains, 1521. I gave him my sealed bond for it to repay the money with thanks on delivery of the bond to me at Nürnberg. I bought a pair of shoes for 6 st. I paid the apothecary 11 st. I paid 3 st. for cord. In Tomasin's kitchen I gave away a Philips fl. in leaving gifts, and I gave the maiden, his daughter, a gold florin as parting present. I have dined with him thrice. To Jobst's wife I gave 1 fl., and another florin in his kitchen for leaving gifts. Also 2 st. paid for lading. Tomasin gave me a jar full of the best Tiriax. I changed 3 fl. for expenses; gave the house servant 10 st. on leaving. I gave Peter 1 st. I have given 2 st. for "trinkgeld"; and 3 st. to Master Jacob's man. I paid 4 st. for canvass. I gave Peter 1 st. Paid the messenger 3 st.

On Our Lady's Visitation, as I was just about to leave Antwerp, the King of Denmark sent to me to come to him at once, and take his portrait, which I did in charcoal. I also did that of his servant Anton, and I was made to dine with the King, and he behaved graciously towards me. I have entrusted my bale to Leonhard Tucher and given over my white cloth to him. The carrier with whom I bargained did not take me,

Master Heinrich. Possibly the painter Herri met de Bles.

Gerhard. Brother of Tomaso Bombelli.

My portrait of the Emperor. The portrait of Emperor Maximilian, that did not please the Regent Marguerite.

King of Denmark. Christian II, King of Denmark from 1484, who married Isabel, sister of Charles V. He resided in Lierre. See Plate 63.

Anton. Anthony von Metz, Danish Ambassador.

Leonhard Tucher. Burgomaster of Nuremberg (1468-1568).

My white cloth. Dürer obtained this in exchange for his portrait of Emperor Maximilian.

I fell out with him. Gerhard gave me some Italian seeds. I gave the new Vicarius, the great turtle shell, the fish-shield, the long pipe, the long weapon, the fish-fins, and the two little casks of lemons and capers to take home for me, on the day of Our Lady's Visitation 1521.

Next day we travelled to Brussels at the command of the King of Denmark, and I engaged a driver to whom I gave 2 fl. I gave the King of Denmark the best of all my prints; they are worth 5 fl. I again changed 2 fl. for expenses. Paid 1 st. for a dish and baskets. I noticed how the people of Antwerp marvelled greatly when they saw the King of Denmark, to find him such a manly, handsome man and come hither through his enemy's land with only two attendants. I saw too how the Emperor rode forth from Brussels to meet him and received him honourably with great pomp. Then I saw the noble, costly banquet, which the Emperor and Lady Margaret held next day in his honour. I bought a pair of gloves for 2 st.

Herr Anton paid me 12 Horn fl., of which I gave the painter 2 Horn fl. for the tablet to paint the portrait on and for having colours rubbed for me. The other 8 Horn fl. I used for expenses.

On the Sunday before Margaret's the King of Denmark gave a great banquet to the Emperor, Lady Margaret, and the Queen of Spain, and he bade me in and I dined there also.

I paid 12 st. for the King's frame, and I painted the King's portrait in oil; he has given me 30 fl. I gave 2 st. to the lad, Bartholomaeus by name, who rubbed the colours for me.

I bought a little glass jar, which once belonged to the King, for 2 st. I gave 2 st. for "trinkgeld". Paid 2 st. for the engraved goblets. I gave Master Jan's boy 4 half-sheets; I also gave the Master-painter's lad an "Apocalypse" and 4 half-sheets.

The Bolognese has given me an Italian work of art, I have

The final page of Manuscript B.　State Archives, Nuremberg (S.I., L 79, No. 15).

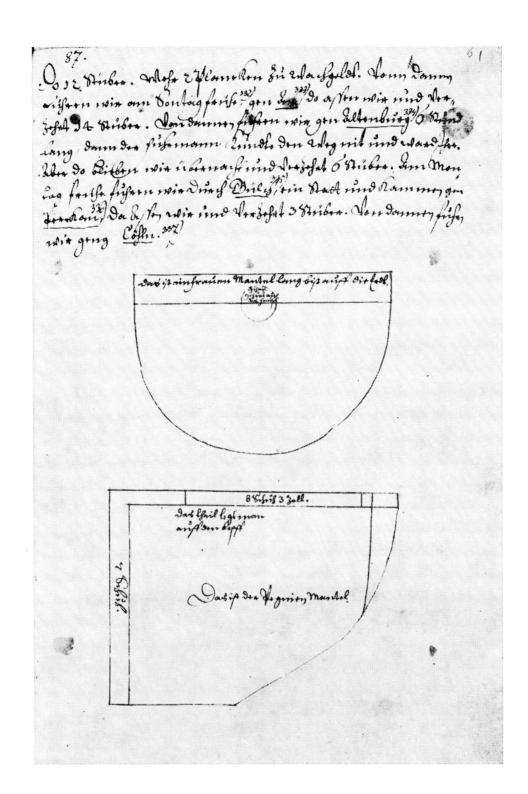

The final page of Manuscript A.   State Library, Bamberg (J.H. Msc. art. 1).

also bought a work for 1 st. Master Jobst the tailor invited me and I supped with him. I paid 32 st. for hire of a room for 8 days at Brussels. I gave an engraved "Passion" to the wife of Master Jan, the goldsmith, with whom I have dined three times. I gave another "Life of Our Lady" to the painter's apprentice Bartholomaeus. I dined with Herr Nicolaus Ziegler and gave 1 st. to Master Jan's servant. I have stayed on at Brussels two days longer on account of a carriage because I could get none. I bought a pair of socks for 1 st.

Master Jan. The goldsmith who deceived Dürer.

On Friday morning early we set off from Brussels, and I am to pay the driver 10 fl. I paid my hostess 5 st. further for the single night. We passed through two villages and came to Louvain, breakfasted and spent 13 st. Then we went through three villages and came to Thienen, which is a small town. There we stopped for the night and I spent 9 st.

We set off thence early on S. Margaret's day and passed thro' two villages and came to a town called S. Truyen where they are building a new, large, and very artistic church tower. From thence we went on past some poor huts and came to a town, Tongres, where we had breakfast and I spent 6 st. Thence we went through a village and some poor houses and came to Maastricht. There I stayed the night and spent 12 st. and 2 "Blanke" besides for watchmoney.

We went early thence on Sunday to Aachen. We ate there and spent 14 st. Thence we travelled a 6-hour stage to Altenburg, for the driver did not know the way and went wrong. There however we stopped for the night and spent 6 st.

Early on Monday we travelled through Juliers, a town, and came to Bergheim where we ate and spent 3 st. Thence we travelled to Köln.

THE SILVERPOINT
SKETCHBOOK

I

2

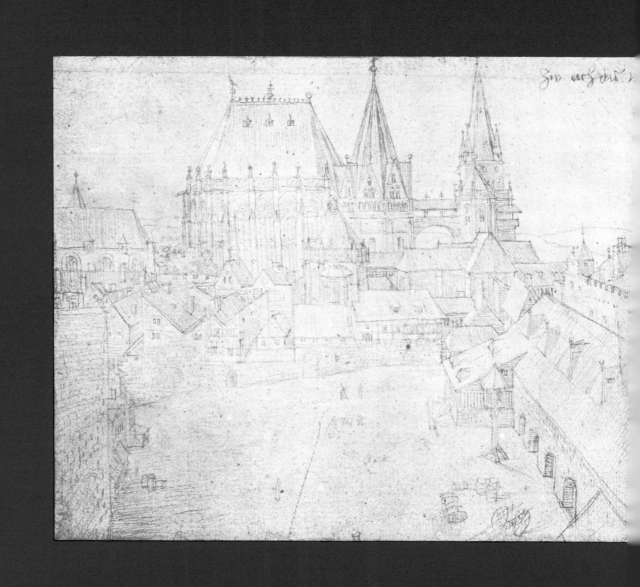

3

5

6

7

8

II

12

13

14

16

17

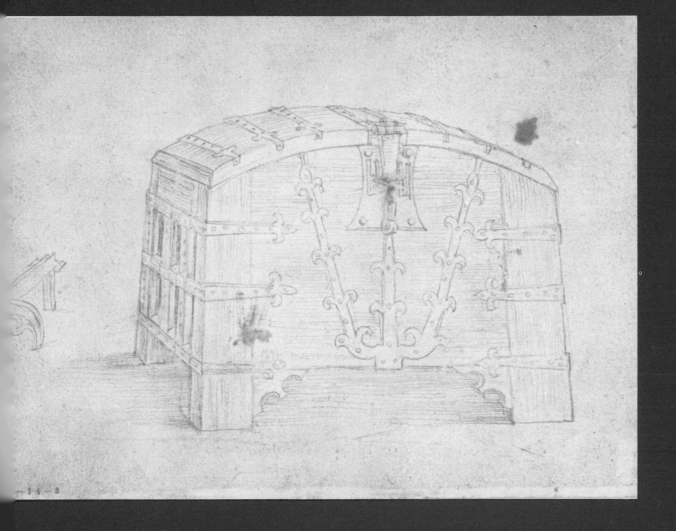

21

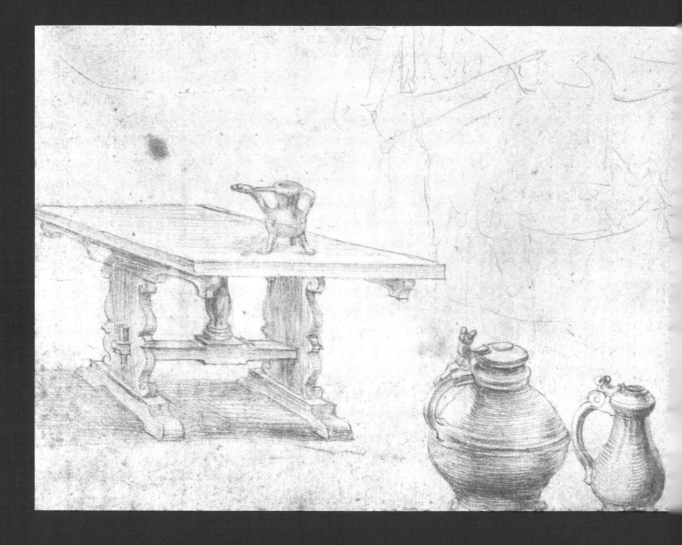

22

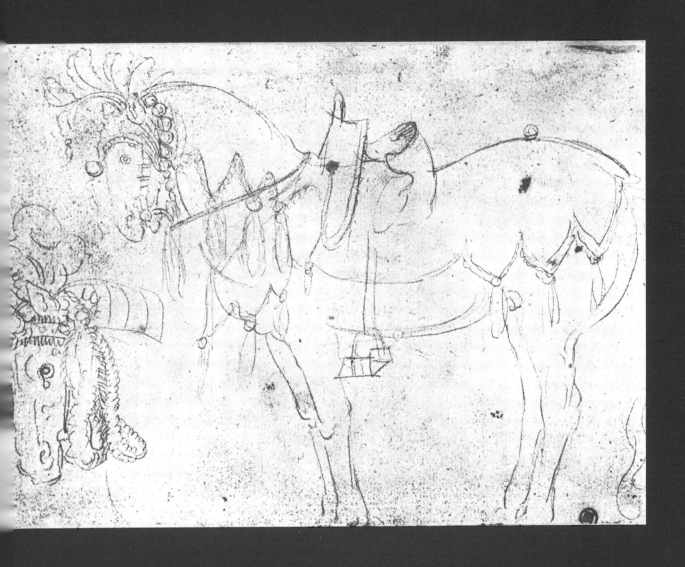

23

no 12. f. 43. 8 L. br. 5 h. g L.

22.

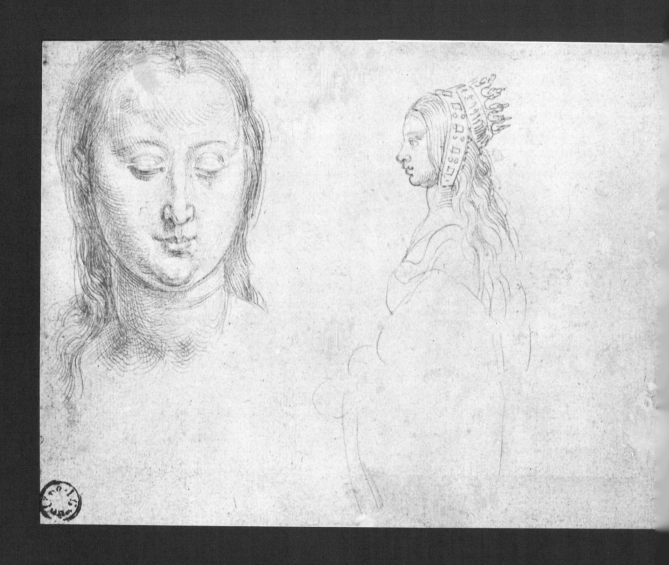

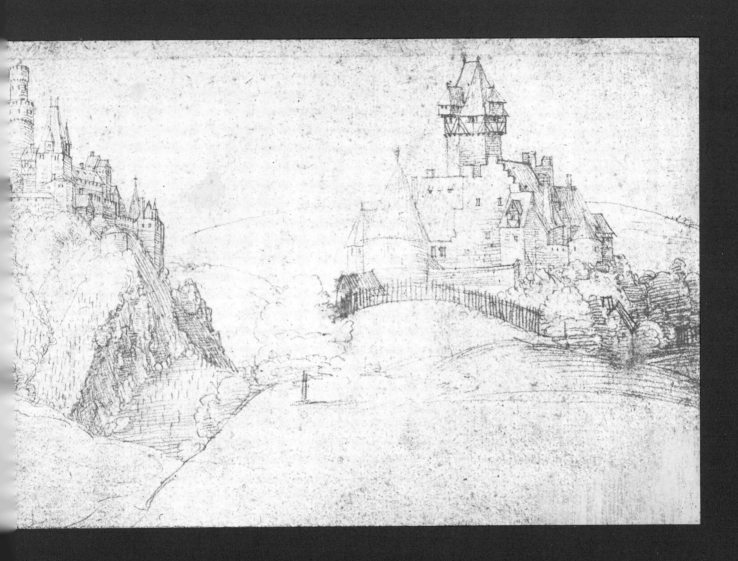

DRAWINGS
AND WATER-COLOURS

28

30

31

32

33 34

38 40

39 41 42

43

44

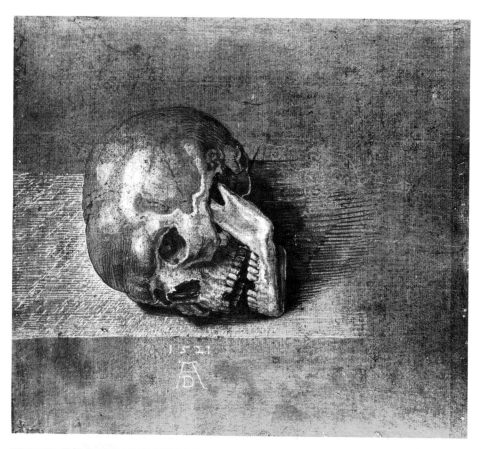

46

47

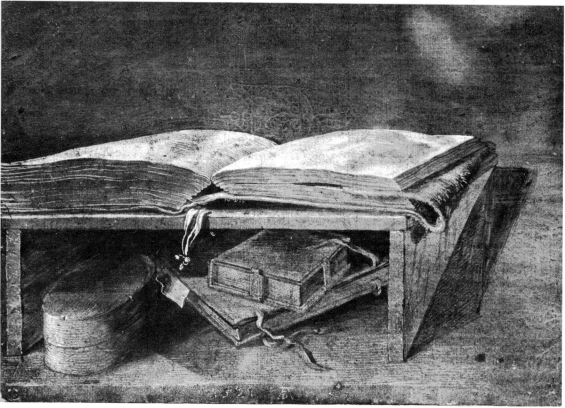

49

50

51 52

53

54

55

56

57

58

59

60

62
61
63

64

65

66

FELIX·HVNGERSPERG

68

70

71

73

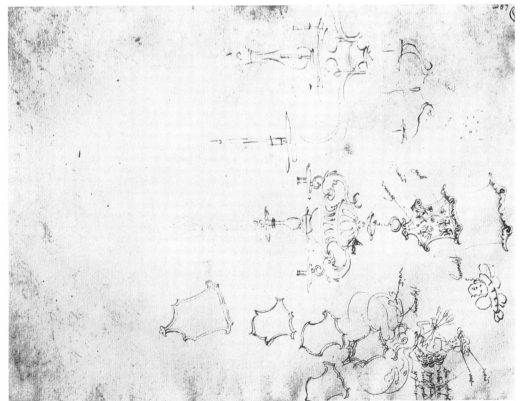

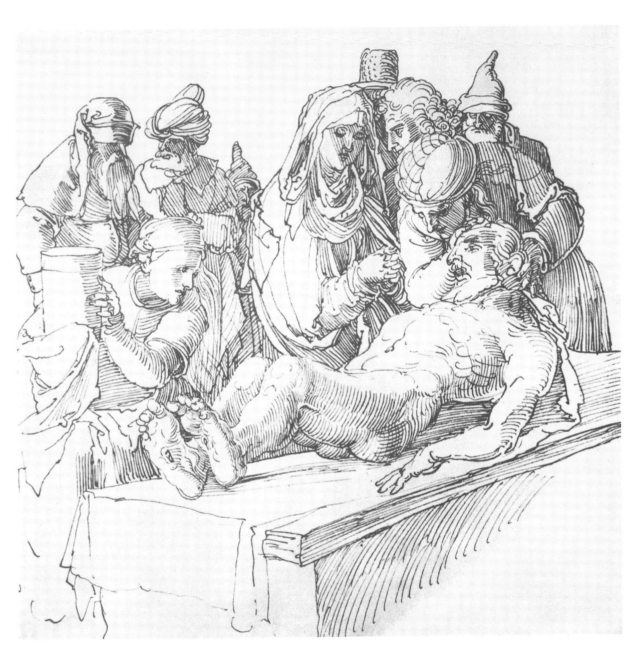

84

85

86

LIST OF ILLUSTRATIONS

PAINTINGS

I SAINT JEROME (page 25).
Oil on wood. 60 × 48 cm. Signed with monogram and dated : *1521*, bottom left. Painted March 1521 in Antwerp. See Diary, page 84, and the preparatory studies, Plates 43 to 47.
Museum of Fine Arts, Lisbon.

II BERNHARD VON RESTEN (page 33).
Oil on oak. 45.5 × 31.5 cm. Signed with monogram and dated : *1521*, above. Inscribed on the letter : *Dem Pernhar... zw...* Painted March 1521 in Antwerp. See Diary, page 85.
Gemäldegalerie, Dresden.

III LORENZ STERCK (page 45).
Oil on canvas. 51 × 32 cm. Signed with monogram and dated : *1521*, above. Painted in Antwerp. See Diary, page 90.
Isabella Stewart Gardner Museum, Boston, Mass.

THE SILVERPOINT SKETCHBOOK

1 PAULUS TOPLER AND MARTIN PFINZING.
Silverpoint. 12.8 × 19 cm. Inscribed by Dürer top centre : *pawll dopler 1520 LXI jor Altt;* and top right : *merten pfintzing XX jor alt;* and lower right : *zw ach gemacht;* and signed twice with monogram. Drawn October 1520 in Aachen. See Diary, page 70.
Print Room, Berlin.

2 AACHEN CATHEDRAL.
Silverpoint. 12.6 × 17.7 cm. Inscribed by Dürer top right : *zw ach das münstr.* Drawn October 1520. See Diary, page 70.
British Museum, London.

3 AACHEN TOWN-HALL.
Silverpoint. 12.7 × 18.9 cm. Inscribed by Dürer top right : *dz rathus zw ach.* Drawn October 1520.
Musée Condé, Chantilly.

4 CASPAR STURM; RIVER LANDSCAPE.
Silverpoint. *Verso* of preceding drawing. Inscribed by Dürer above : *1520 CASPER STVRM ALT 45 Jor zw ach gemacht;* and below : *toll (?).* See Diary, pages 70 and 75.

5 A DOG LYING DOWN.
Silverpoint. 12.3 × 17.5 cm. Inscribed by Dürer top right : *zw ach gemacht;* and signed with monogram. Drawn October 1520 in Aachen.
British Museum, London.

6 TWO STUDIES OF COSTUMES.
Silverpoint. *Verso* of the preceding drawing. The figure on the left is copied after a bronze statuette by Jacques Gérines

(Rijksmuseum, Amsterdam) from the Tomb of Joanna of Brabant in the Carmelite Church in Brussels, and represents Marie de Bourgogne. The figure on the right appears again on a drawing with the inscription : "*ein türgin*" (see Plate 35).

7 PORTRAIT OF A MAN OF TWENTY-FOUR YEARS; THE ABBEY OF SAINT MICHAEL, ANTWERP.
Silverpoint. 13.3 × 19.4 cm. Inscribed by Dürer top left : *1520 XXIIII;* and top right : *sant michell zw antorff.* See Diary, page 60.
Musée Condé, Chantilly.

8 VIEW OF BERGEN-OP-ZOOM.
Silverpoint. *Verso* of the preceding drawing. Inscribed by Dürer above : *zw pergen.* Drawn December 1520. See Diary, page 77.

9 JAN DE HAS' SERVANT AND AN ELDERLY WOMAN.
Silverpoint. 12.9 × 19 cm. Inscribed by Dürer top left : *zw pergen. feuertag (?).* Drawn December 1520 in Bergen-op-Zoom. See Diary, page 77.
Musée Condé, Chantilly.

10 A WOMAN OF BERGEN-OP-ZOOM AND A WOMAN OF TER GOES.
Silverpoint. *Verso* of the preceding drawing. Inscribed by Dürer top left : *zw pergen;* and top right : *zw der gus in selant.* Drawn December 1520. See Diary, page 77.

11 THE CHOIR OF THE GROOTE KERK, BERGEN-OP-ZOOM.
Silverpoint. 13.2 × 18.2 cm. Inscribed by Dürer above : *Dz ist der new kor zw pergen.* Drawn December 1520.
Städelsches Kunstinstitut, Frankfurt.

12 MARX ULSTAT; THE BEAUTIFUL YOUNG LADY OF ANTWERP.
Silverpoint. *Verso* of the preceding drawing. Inscribed by Dürer top left : *marx ulstat den hab ich awff dr se conterfet;* and top right : *dy schon Jungfer zw antorf 1521.* The young lady was apparently Gerhard Bombelli's fiancée. The number *18*, which appears twice, apparently indicates her age.

13 LAZARUS RAVENSBURGER; THE TOWER OF LIERE PALACE IN ANTWERP.
Silverpoint. 12.2 × 16.9 cm. Inscribed by Dürer above : *... rus (?) rafenspurger ... gemacht zw antorff.*
Print Room, Berlin.

14 A YOUNG GIRL IN NETHERLANDISH COSTUME.
Silverpoint. *Verso* of the preceding drawing.

15 A CARDINAL SEATED ON A THRONE; A MAN IN A FUR CAP.
Silverpoint. 12.7 × 18.4 cm.
Print Room, Berlin.

16 STUDIES OF A DOG AND LION.
Silverpoint. *Verso* of the preceding drawing. Inscribed by Dürer top left : *zw antorff*.

17 A MAN OF ANTWERP; VIEW NEAR ANDERNACH.
Silverpoint. 12.2 × 17.1 cm. Inscribed by Dürer top left : *zw antorff 1521*; and top right : *pey andernach am (?) rein*. The landscape was drawn on Dürer's return journey in July 1521. See Diary, page 97.
Print Room, Berlin.

18 TWO LIONS.
Silverpoint. *Verso* of the preceding drawing. Probably drawn April 1521 in Ghent. See Diary, page 87.

19 A LION.
Silverpoint. 12.9 × 19 cm. Inscribed by Dürer above : *zw gent*. Drawn April 1521 in Ghent. See Diary, page 87.
Albertina, Vienna.

20 YOUNG GIRL IN A COLOGNE HEAD-DRESS; AGNES DÜRER ON THE RHINE NEAR BOPPARD.
Silverpoint. *Verso* of the preceding drawing. Inscribed by Dürer top left : *Cölnisch gepend*; and top right : *awff dem rin mein weib pey popart*. Drawn on Dürer's return journey in July 1521.

21 A TRUNK.
Silverpoint. 11.5 × 16.7 cm.
British Museum, London.

22 A TABLE AND JUGS; SKETCH OF A HORSE.
Silverpoint. *Verso* of the preceding drawing.

23 STUDIES OF A CAPARISONED HORSE.
Silverpoint. 12.5 × 18 cm.
Germanisches Nationalmuseum, Nuremberg (Depositum I. Petersen).

24 TILED PAVEMENTS; TWO HANDS HOLDING A LITTLE DOG.
Silverpoint. *Verso* of the preceding drawing.

25 A MORTAR.
Silverpoint. 12.7 × 18.3 cm. Below right, a 19th-century catalogue reference. Probably drawn on the 6th June 1521 in the house of the gun-founder Hans Poppenreuter in Malines.
Formerly in the Kunsthalle, Bremen.

26 HEAD OF A YOUNG GIRL; A YOUNG GIRL, WEARING A CROWN, IN PROFILE.
Silverpoint. *Verso* of the preceding drawing.

27 THE CASTLE OF RHEINFELS, NEAR SANKT GOAR; AND ANOTHER CASTLE ON THE RHINE (STOLZENFELS?).
Silverpoint. 11 × 17.8 cm. Drawn on the return journey in July 1521.
Germanisches Nationalmuseum, Nuremberg (Depositum I. Petersen).

THE BOOK OF PEN SKETCHES

28 A GOLDSMITH OF MALINES.
Pen. 15.9 × 10.1 cm. Inscribed by Dürer above : *ein goltschmit von mechell zw antorff gemacht 1520*; and signed with monogram on the right. Possibly a portrait of Stefan Capello. See Diary, page 77.
Print Room, Berlin.

29 JOBST PLANKFELT.
Pen. 15.8 × 10.6 cm. Inscribed by Dürer above : *Das ist mein wirt zw antorf jobst blankfelt 1520*. Signed with monogram on the right.
Städelsches Kunstinstitut, Frankfurt.

30 A WOMAN OF BRUSSELS.
Pen. 16 × 10.5 cm. Inscribed by Dürer above : *1520 zw prussel gemacht*; and signed with monogram. Possibly a portrait of the god-mother of the wife of Dürer's host in Brussels. See Diary, page 65.
Albertina, Vienna.

31 PORTRAIT OF CAPTAIN FELIX HUNGERSBERG.
Pen. 16 × 10.5 cm. Inscribed by Dürer on the left : *Das ist hawbt man felix der köstlich lavten schlaher*; and above right : *zw antorff gemacht*; and signed with monogram and dated : *1520*, on the right. See Diary, page 59; and see Plate 67.
Albertina, Vienna.

32 HANS PFAFFROTH VON DANZIG.
Pen. 16.1 × 10.8 cm. Inscribed by Dürer above : *hans pfaffrot von danczgen 1520 ein starckman*; and signed with monogram on the right. See Diary, page 60.
Collection E. de Rothschild, Paris.

33 PORTRAIT OF A BEARDED MAN.
Pen. 16 × 11.4 cm. Above right, Dürer's monogram added by another hand.
Städelsches Kunstinstitut, Frankfurt.

34 A WOMAN IN THE POSE OF A 'MATER DOLOROSA'.
Pen. 15.1 × 10.4 cm. Inscribed by Dürer above : *awff dem rein gemacht*, and : *1521*. Dürer's monogram added by another hand.
Germanisches Nationalmuseum, Nuremberg.

35 A TURKISH WOMAN.
Pen. 18.1 × 10.6 cm. Inscribed by Dürer above : *ein türgin*; and Dürer's monogram added by another hand on the right. The same figure appears in the Silverpoint Sketchbook (Plate 6).
Ambrosiana, Milan.

36 AN OARSMAN.
Pen. 16 × 10.3 cm.
Formerly in the Lubomirski Museum, Lemberg.

37 ARNOLD VON SELIGENSTADT.
Pen. 12.3 × 9.9 cm. Inscribed by Dürer top right : *meistr ornolt von d. selgenstat 1520;* and signed with monogram. Musée Bonnat, Bayonne.

38 PROFILE PORTRAIT OF AN OLD MAN.
Pen. 8.3 × 11.2 cm. Dated by Dürer above : *1521;* and with Dürer's monogram added by another hand. Albertina, Vienna.

39 A YOUNG MAN SINGING.
Pen. 11.3 × 9 cm. Dated by Dürer top right : *1521.* Print Room, Berlin.

40 BUST OF AN ORIENTAL.
Pen. 10.7 × 5.7 cm. Dated by Dürer above : *1521.* Print Room, Berlin.

41 NUDE FIGURE OF A YOUNG MAN, BUST-LENGTH (SAINT SEBASTIAN?).
Pen. 10.3 × 8 cm.
British Museum, London.

42 AN OLD MAN WITH A BEARD.
Pen. 9.4 × 8 cm.
British Museum, London.

DRAWINGS AND WATER-COLOURS

43 AN OLD MAN OF 93 YEARS.
Brush drawing in black, heightened in white, on paper given a violet ground. 42 × 28.2 cm. Inscribed by Dürer above : *Der man was alt 93 jor vnd noch gesund vnd vermuglich zw antorff.* Signed with monogram and dated : *1521,* above left. This is probably the man to whom Dürer gave 3 deniers for sitting for him in the early part of the year 1521 (see Diary, page 80). It was used as a preparatory study of Saint Jerome (see Plate I, page 25).
Albertina, Vienna.

44 HEAD OF AN OLD MAN OF 93 YEARS.
Brush drawing in black, heightened in white, on paper given a violet ground. 26.9 × 20 cm. Signed with monogram and dated : *1521,* top left. Like the preceding drawing, used as a preparatory study for the painting of Saint Jerome (Plate I, page 25).
Print Room, Berlin.

45 STUDIES FOR THE LEFT HAND AND ARM OF SAINT JEROME.
Brush drawing in black, heightened in white, on paper given a violet ground. 39.5 × 28.6 cm. Signed with monogram and dated : *1521,* below. Preparatory study for the painting of Saint Jerome (Plate I, page 25).
Albertina, Vienna.

46 A BOOK-REST AND BOOKS.
Brush drawing in black, heightened in white, on paper given a violet ground. 19.8 × 28 cm. Signed with monogram and dated : *1521,* below. Preparatory study for the painting of Saint Jerome (Plate I, page 25).
Albertina, Vienna.

47 A SKULL.
Brush drawing in black, heightened in white, on paper given a violet ground. 18 × 19.2 cm. The skull that Dürer bought for 2 pfennigs was possibly the model for this drawing (see Diary, page 71). Preparatory study for the painting of Saint Jerome (Plate I, page 25).
Albertina, Vienna.

48 SAINT CHRISTOPHER.
Pen and black ink, heightened in white, on paper given a violet ground. 18.5 × 14 cm. Possibly one of the "*4 Christophel awff graw papir*" drawn in May 1521 for Joachim Patinir (see Diary, page 93; and see Plate 90).
British Museum, London.

49 RODRIGO FERNANDEZ D'ALMADA.
Brush drawing in black, heightened in white, on paper given a violet ground. 37.3 × 27.1 cm. Drawn in April 1521 in Antwerp. See Diary, page 62.
Print Room, Berlin.

50 AGNES DÜRER IN NETHERLANDISH DRESS.
Drawing on paper given a violet ground. 40.7 × 27.1 cm. An old inscription above reads : *Das hat albrecht dürer nach seiner hawsfrawen Conterfet zw antorff inder niderlendischen kleidung im jor 1521 Do sy aneinander zw der e gehabt hetten XXVII jor* (portrait of his wife drawn by Dürer in 1521 in Antwerp after they had been married for 27 years).
Print Room, Berlin.

51 A WOMAN IN NETHERLANDISH DRESS.
Brush drawing in black, heightened in white, on paper given a violet ground. 28.3 × 19.5 cm. Signed with monogram and dated : *1521,* top right. Drawn at the end of May or beginning of June 1521 in Antwerp (see Diary, page 94).
National Gallery, Washington D.C.

52 COSTUME STUDY.
Brush drawing in black, heightened in white, on paper given a violet ground. 28 × 21 cm. Signed with monogram and dated : *1521,* top right. Drawn at the end of May or the beginning of June 1521 in Antwerp (see Diary, page 94).
Albertina, Vienna.

53 PORTRAIT OF A YOUNG MAN.
Charcoal. 36.5 × 25.8 cm. Signed with monogram and dated : *1520,* above.
Print Room, Berlin.

54 PORTRAIT OF A YOUNG MAN.
Charcoal. 41.2 × 27.4 cm. Signed with monogram above and dated : *1520.*
Musée du Louvre, Paris.

55 ERASMUS OF ROTTERDAM.
Charcoal. 37.3 × 27.1 cm. Dated by Dürer : *1521*, above; and inscribed in pen in another hand : *Erasmus fon rottertam.* Probably the portrait drawn by Dürer at the end of August 1520 in Brussels (see Diary, page 65). The charcoal portrait is mentioned by Erasmus in a letter dated the 8th January 1525 addressed to Willibald Pirckheimer.
Musée du Louvre, Paris.

56 PORTRAIT OF A YOUNG MAN.
Charcoal. 36.7 × 26.4 cm. Signed with monogram and dated : *1521*, above.
Formerly in the Schlossmuseum, Weimar.

57 PORTRAIT OF A MAN (JACOPO DEI BANISSI).
Charcoal. 34 × 30 cm. Probably drawn in September 1520 in Antwerp. See Diary, page 67.
Rijksmuseum, Amsterdam.

58 PORTRAIT OF A YOUNG MAN.
Charcoal. 37.8 × 27.3 cm. Dated by Dürer : *1521*, above; and with Dürer's monogram and the date *1521* added by another hand, below.
British Museum, London.

59 BERNARD VAN ORLEY (?).
Charcoal. 41 × 28.2 cm. Signed with monogram and dated : *1521*, above; and inscribed in another hand : *eghenn handt* (his own hand). Dürer mentions making a portrait of "Master Bernard" in charcoal in August 1520 (see Diary, page 65).
Collection E. de Rothschild, Paris.

60 PORTRAIT OF A MAN.
Charcoal. 36.8 × 25.5 cm. Inscribed bottom left with Lukas van Leyden's monogram and the year *1525*; and : "*Effigies Lucae Leidensis*". There are traces of Dürer's monogram and the date *1521*.
British Museum, London.

61 PORTRAIT OF A WOMAN WITH A NETHER-LANDISH HEAD-DRESS.
Charcoal. 40 × 28.1 cm. Signed with monogram and dated : *1521*, above.
British Museum, London.

62 PORTRAIT OF A MAN (NICLAS KRATZER?).
Charcoal (?). 37.1 × 27.8 cm.
Collection E. de Rothschild, Paris.

63 PORTRAIT OF CHRISTIAN II, KING OF DENMARK.
Charcoal. 40 × 28.7 cm. Signed with monogram and dated : *1521*, above. Drawn on the 2nd July 1521 in Brussels (see Diary, page 99).
British Museum, London.

64 SEBASTIAN BRANT (?).
Silverpoint. 19.4 × 14.7 cm. (The drawing has been cut out and mounted on a sheet of paper). If it is a portrait of Sebastian Brant it will have been made in August 1520 in Antwerp.
Print Room, Berlin.

65 LUKAS VAN LEYDEN.
Silverpoint. 24.4 × 17.1 cm. Signed with monogram above, and inscribed in another hand, below left : *Alberto D...* Drawn June 1521 in Antwerp (see Diary, page 96).
Musée Wicar, Lille.

66 PORTRAIT OF BRANDÂO'S MOORISH SERVANT, CATHERINA.
Silverpoint. 20 × 14 cm. Inscribed by Dürer : *1521 Katharina allt 20 jar*, above; and signed with monogram. Drawn in March or April 1521 in Antwerp (see Diary, page 85).
Uffizi, Florence.

67 PORTRAIT OF FELIX HUNGERSBERG KNEELING.
Pen. 27.8 × 20.8 cm. Inscribed by Dürer (?), above : *FELIX. HVNGERSPERG Der kostlich vnd vbergrad lawtenschlaher;* and on the right : *Das sind dy pesten Felix adolff samario.* Drawn November 1520 in Antwerp (see Diary, page 77; and see Plate 31).
Albertina, Vienna.

68 THE PORT OF ANTWERP NEAR THE SCHELDT TOWER.
Pen. 21.3 × 28.3 cm. Inscribed by Dürer : *1520 Antorff*, above.
Albertina, Vienna.

69 IRISH WARRIORS AND PEASANTS.
Pen and water-colour. 21 × 28.2 cm. Inscribed by Dürer, top left : *Also gand dy krigs man in Irlandia hinder engeland;* and top right : *Also gand dy pawern in Irlandyen;* and signed with monogram and dated : *1521*, top centre.
Print Room, Berlin.

70 TWO LIVONIAN WOMEN.
Pen and water-colour. 19.1 × 20.1 cm. Inscribed by Dürer above : *In eyflant gett das gemein folg also.*
Collection E. de Rothschild, Paris.

71 THREE DISTINGUISHED LIVONIAN WOMEN.
Pen and water-colour. 18.7 × 19.7 cm. Inscribed by Dürer above : *also gat man in Eyflant dy mechtigen;* and signed with monogram and date : *1521*.
Collection E. de Rothschild, Paris.

72 A WEALTHY LIVONIAN WOMAN.
Pen and water-colour. 27.5 × 18.5 cm. Inscribed by Dürer top left : *Also gand dy reichen frawen in eiffland;* and signed with monogram and dated : *1521*.
Collection E. de Rothschild, Paris.

73 HEAD OF A WALRUS.
Pen and water-colour. 20.6 × 31.5 cm. Inscribed by Dürer top left : *1521 Das dosig thyr van dem ich das hawbt conterfett hab, ist gefangen worden in der niderlendischen see vnd was XII ellen lang brawendisch mit für füssen;* and signed with monogram.
British Museum, London.

74 LANDSCAPE AND ANIMAL STUDIES.
Pen, with some water-colour (in the baboon). 26.7 × 37.9 cm. Signed with monogram and dated *1520*, above right; and inscribed : *ein sunder tier das Ich ... gros anderthalben czentn*(er) *schw* (er).
Sterling and Francine Clark Art Institute, Williamstown, Virginia.

75 THE ANIMAL PARK IN BRUSSELS.
Pen. 28.3 × 40 cm. Inscribed by Dürer and dated : *1520*, above; and inscribed : *Dz ist zw prüsell der diergarten vnd dis lust hinden aws dem schlos hinab zw sehen.* Drawn at the end of August 1520 (see Diary, page 63).
Academy of Fine Arts, Vienna.

76 CHRIST ON THE MOUNT OF OLIVES.
Pen. 20.6 × 27.4 cm. Signed with monogram and dated : *1520*, bottom left.
Collection R. von Hirsch, Basle.

77 CHRIST ON THE MOUNT OF OLIVES.
Pen. 20.8 × 29.4 cm. Below the figure of Christ, on the left, signed with monogram and dated : *1521*. Probably one of the "*2 ölberg*" drawn by Dürer in May 1521 (see Diary, page 94). On the *verso* is the drawing reproduced on Plate 79.
Städelsches Kunstinstitut, Frankfurt.

78 CHRIST ON THE MOUNT OF OLIVES.
Pen. 16.1 × 16.8 cm. Inscribed below in another hand : *albert duer hant selw* (Dürer's own hand).
Print Room, Berlin.

79 STUDIES OF COATS-OF-ARMS AND A HANGING LAMP.
Pen. 20.8 × 29.4 cm. The *verso* of the drawing reproduced on Plate 77. Dürer's inscriptions accompany the coats-of-arms. Probably the arms of the Englishman whom Dürer met in May or June 1521 (see Diary, page 94).

80 CHRIST CARRYING THE CROSS.
Pen. 21 × 28.5 cm. Signed with monogram and dated : *1520*, below.
Uffizi, Florence.

81 CHRIST CARRYING THE CROSS.
Pen. 21 × 28.5 cm. Signed with monogram and dated : *1520*, below.
Uffizi, Florence.

82 THE CRUCIFIXION.
Pen. 32.3 × 22.3 cm. Signed with monogram and dated : *1521*, on the base of the Cross.
Albertina, Vienna.

83 THE BEWAILING OF CHRIST.
Pen. 29 × 21 cm. Signed with monogram and dated : *1521*, above.
Fogg Art Museum, Cambridge, Mass.

84 THE ENTOMBMENT.
Pen. 20.4 × 20.7 cm.
Formerly in the Lubomirski Museum, Lemberg.

85 THE CARRYING OF CHRIST'S BODY TO THE TOMB.
Pen. 20.5 × 29 cm. Signed with monogram and dated : *1521*, bottom left.
Uffizi, Florence.

86 THE CARRYING OF CHRIST'S BODY TO THE TOMB.
Pen. 21 × 28.9 cm. Signed with monogram and dated : *1521*, bottom left.
Germanisches Nationalmuseum, Nuremberg.

87 THE VIRGIN AND CHILD ON A BANK, WITH A MUSIC-MAKING ANGEL.
Pen. 24.2 × 20.7 cm. Dated by Dürer : *1520*, above; and below this, Dürer's monogram added by another hand.
Kunsthalle, Hamburg.

88 SAINT JEROME.
Pen. 20.2 × 12.5 cm. Below, Dürer's monogram added by another hand.
Print Room, Berlin.

89 A WOMAN KNEELING IN PRAYER.
Pen. 16.1 × 10.1 cm. On the *prie-dieu* and again top right, Dürer's monograms added by another hand.
Formerly in the Kunsthalle, Bremen.

90 NINE STUDIES FOR A SAINT CHRISTOPHER.
Pen. 22.8 × 40.7 cm. Signed with monogram and dated : *1521*, above. Probably made in connection with the "*4 Christophel awff graw papir*" that Dürer drew for Joachim Patinir in May 1521. See Diary, page 93; and see Plate 48.
Print Room, Berlin.

LIST OF ILLUSTRATIONS

PHOTOGRAPHIC ACKNOWLEDGMENTS

Albertina, Vienna : 19, 20, 30, 31, 38, 43, 45, 46, 47, 52, 67, 68, 82. Busch-Hanck, Frankfurt / M. : 11, 12. Gabinetto Fotografico, Florence : 66, 80, 81, 85. Studio Gérondal, Lille : 65. Giraudon, Paris : 3, 4, 7, 8, 9, 10. Jacqueline Hyde, Paris : 32, 54, 55, 59, 62, 70, 71, 72. Kleinhempel, Hamburg : 87. Foto-Commissie Rijksmuseum, Amsterdam : 57. Walter Steinkopf, Berlin : 13, 14, 15, 16, 17, 18, 28, 39, 40, 44, 49, 50, 53, 64, 78, 89, 90. Stickelmann, Bremen : 25, 26.

Printed in Belgium.
By LACONTI s.a., Brussels
Offset films by Etabl. TALLON, Brussels
Binding by Presses SAINT-AUGUSTIN, Bruges.

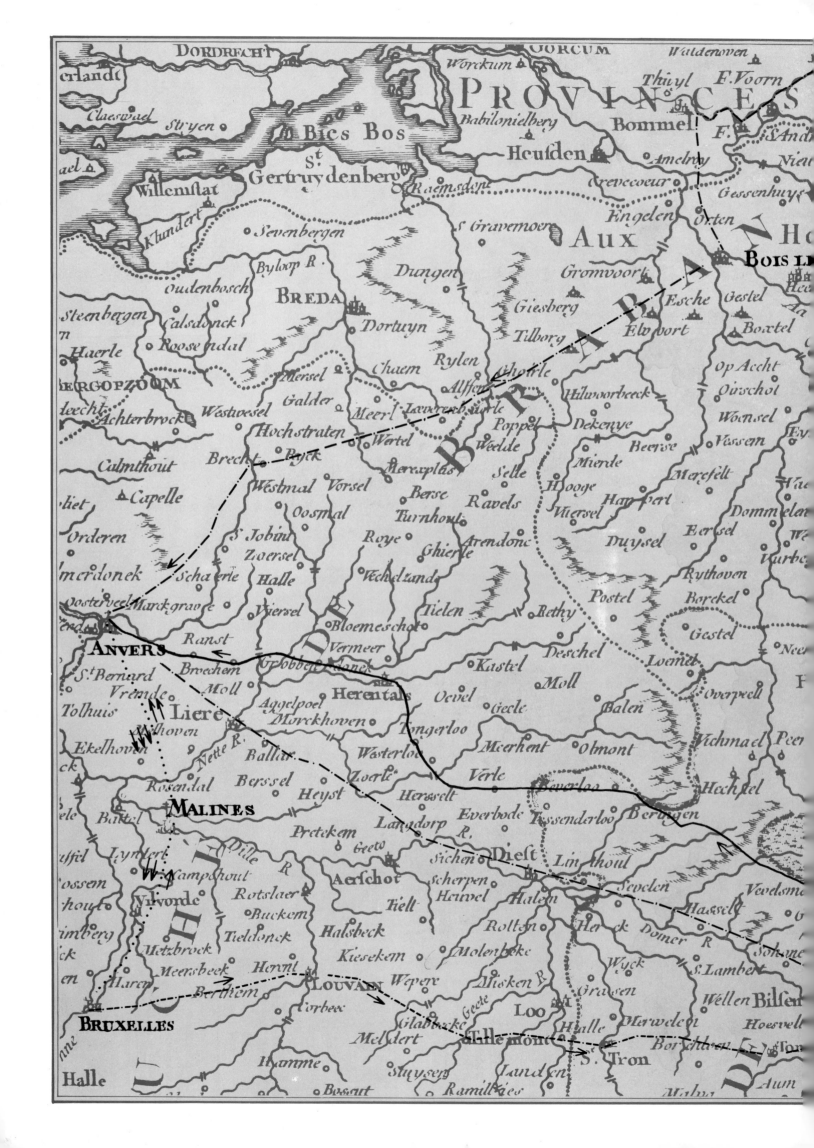